GUY GONE KETO

07|23|20

Amir —

Thank you So So much
for your Support.
I'm Grateful to have you
in my orbit.
Go Keto!

th——

GUY GONE KETO

How to Lose Weight, Feel Great,
and Achieve Lifelong Fitness

———

THOM KING

LIONCREST

PUBLISHING

GUY GONE KETO

How to Lose Weight, Feel Great, and Achieve Lifelong Fitness

ISBN   978-1-5445-1098-9 *Paperback*
      978-1-5445-1097-2 *Ebook*

CONTENTS

INTRODUCTION............................. 11

PART I: GOING KETO

1. YO-YO WEIGHT............................. 29
2. THE KETOGENIC DIET 45

PART II: KNOW THY LABEL

3. SO MUCH SUGAR............................ 67
4. GO NATURALLY SWEET 97

PART III: LET'S EAT

5. KETO MEAL PLAN...........................113
6. GOOD CHEATS.............................155

CONCLUSION...............................165
EPILOGUE.................................181
ACKNOWLEDGEMENTS 183
ABOUT THE AUTHOR 187

Before you start any lifestyle change, I urge you to talk with your doctor. That's what I did.

I have used my best efforts in writing *Guy Gone Keto*. The information is provided "as is." I make no representation or warranties with respect to the accuracy or completeness of the contents of the cookbook section, and I specifically disclaim any implied warranties of merchantability or fitness for any particular purpose.

All material in *Guy Gone Keto* is provided for your information only and may not be construed as medical advice or instruction. No action or inaction should be taken based solely on the contents of this information; instead, readers should consult appropriate health professionals on any matter relating to their health and well-being.

In the end, I'm just a guy who's gone keto. That's about the extent of it. I AM NOT NOR DO I CLAIM TO BE A DOCTOR, NUTRITIONIST OR DIETITIAN. THE INFORMATION IN GUY GONE KETO IS MERELY MY PERSONAL EXPERIENCES AND OPINION AND DOES NOT REPLACE PROFESSIONAL MEDICAL OR NUTRITIONAL ADVICE.

INTRODUCTION

I woke up in a suite at the Luxor Hotel in Las Vegas. I felt terrible.

I was in town for a trade show, and the night before, a client had taken me to dinner. We had ordered these massive, hundred-dollar steaks, drunk several glasses of wine, and gorged ourselves on ice cream for dessert.

I'd brought the leftovers back to the room, and they still sat on the counter. I glanced around the room. Although they had upgraded my room to a suite, the place was run down and sad. There was a Jacuzzi in the middle of the room, and the place reeked of alcohol a previous guest had spilled.

I got out of bed and looked at myself in the full-length mirror. I was six-foot-two, and I weighed 235 pounds. I felt sick. I was flabby and tired and filled with remorse. I was being sued by my first ex-wife, divorcing my second wife, and taking medication for high blood pressure.

As I stood in front of the mirror, I asked myself, "How the hell did I get here?"

The worst of it was that I felt like a liar and a hypocrite. I own a company, Steviva, that promotes healthy products. One of our principles is to help people improve their health and diet by providing them with natural, no-calorie sweeteners to replace the unhealthy refined and man-made sugars that make them sick and overweight.

Yet here I was, a fat flab who did not lead a disciplined life. I ate whatever I wanted whenever I wanted and drank whatever I wanted whenever I wanted to. It wasn't unusual for me to drink half a bottle of wine a night, eat pizza a couple of times a week, and chow down on dessert every night. Food had stopped being sustenance for me and had become an addiction. I was addicted to alcohol. I was addicted to high-glycemic carbohydrates. I was addicted to sugar. I was also addicted to approval. I was drawn into unhealthy, destructive relationships with women, driven by a need to please others.

I turned away from the mirror, disgusted with myself.

TAKING A NEW ROAD

That was my turning point. From that day in September 2016 forward, I vowed to make changes not just to my diet but to my entire lifestyle. I knew it was going to be a difficult journey. I would experience more than a little discomfort as I changed my diet and exercise habits, and as I focused on the changes, I needed to be a better person. I would have to stop associating with certain people. I'd have to give up many of my favorite foods. I'd have to carefully track my progress. However, I vowed to change.

Now, as I write this a year later, I weigh less than two hundred pounds. My blood pressure is normal. I run three and a half miles every morning. My waist size has dropped from thirty-eight to thirty-three. I am more clear-minded, optimistic, and energetic than I have been at any other time in my fifty-seven-year life.

My journey turned out to be more of a marathon than a sprint, and I'm grateful for that. If I'm in a marathon, that means I'm making long-term choices and changes that will stay with me and help me for the rest of my life. I've done sprints before, and I can tell you short-term efforts to lose weight and get fit don't work. You might lose weight, but if your diet and exercise habits are not part of a lifestyle change, you can expect to see your weight spin up and down like a yo-yo. Believe me, I've probably gained and lost thousands of pounds in my adult life.

I'm a huge fan of author and life coach Tony Robbins, who says if you want to change a habit, you must associate massive amounts of pain to that habit. That day in Las Vegas, I meditated on the pain and suffering overindulgence had caused me. I associated my first divorce, my indulgent habits, and certain wrong-headed decisions with my poor lifestyle choices. I spent an hour throwing myself into an enormous pool of agony so these bad habits would no longer be associated with pleasure but with pain and regret.

I realized that if I kept up this lifestyle, I would soon be dead of a heart attack, stroke, or even cancer. I lost both my parents to cancer, and I knew rogue cancer cells present in a person's body eat glucose to survive. I thought of all the sugar I ate and imagined these rogue cancer cells flourishing in my body.

Later, I bought a journal and chronicled my journey from sloth, indulgence, and dishonesty to a life of self-exploration, healthy eating, and the study of the science behind getting healthy and fit.

DISCOVERY, FORGIVENESS, AND TRANSFORMATION

This has been more than a journey of diet and exercise. It's been a journey of self-discovery and self-forgiveness. What started out as a diet and lifestyle change became a complete transformation of who I was.

I surrounded myself with like-minded people and positive role models. It's been said you're the sum of the five people closest to you, and in my case, that meant I was surrounded by people who enabled my overindulgence. So I listened to Tim Ferriss, who wrote the 4-Hour series of books, and Jocko Willink, the ex-Navy Seal who wrote the book *Extreme Ownership*. I read everything I could find by Dr. Dom D'Agostino of the University of South Florida, one of the world's foremost experts on ketogenic diets.

Before long, I was getting up at 4:30 a.m. like Jocko Willink. I went to bed at nine o'clock, cut out wine, and followed a ketogenic diet.

I'd been aware of ketogenic diets for several years, since Dr. Robert Atkins introduced it to the world with his bestseller *Dr. Atkins' Diet Revolution* in 1972. The diet is simple: you eat mostly fat and protein and greatly reduce your consumption of sugar and carbohydrates, particularly refined sugar and white flour.

Although people attacked it at first—we'd all been taught that fatty foods made you fat and that sugary foods gave you energy—more than twenty studies in recent years have shown that low-carbohydrate diets like the ketogenic diet can help you lose weight and get healthier. In 2003, the same year that Dr. Atkins died, the *Harvard Health Letter* said Atkins's diet was hard to discredit.

I learned our bodies burn fat more efficiently than sugars or carbohydrates. When you reduce those sugars and carbs, your body burns the white fat around your organs and around your belly and other places for energy. If you ingest a lot of sugar and carbs and you don't exercise enough to burn those carbohydrates off, your body converts the sugar and carbs to fat. When you get too much of that fat, you see problems with heart disease, diabetes, and organ failure.

Studies show 80 percent of weight loss is attributed to diet and 20 percent to exercise. You can lose weight on a ketogenic diet, but if you go back to your old way of eating, you will gain the weight back. Yo-yoing like that is even harder on your heart than remaining overweight. To succeed in the long term—to live longer with greater health benefits—you need to make a commitment to a lifestyle of eating right and exercising. It's what I did, and I've never regretted it.

YOUR OWN JOURNEY TO HEALTH

My goal with this book is to share my journey to better health so you, too, can make lasting changes. These lifestyle changes will help you forestall the effects of aging and help you fight off the diseases that come from being unhealthy and overweight.

My own experiences have proven these techniques work,

but don't take my word for it. This book is also based on the latest scientific findings that show a diet rich in fats and protein and low in sugars and carbohydrates will not only help you lose weight but will improve your brain function. By following the suggestions in this book, you'll have a better chance of fighting off cancer, diabetes, cardiovascular disease, and dementia. You'll be happier and more productive.

These are lofty goals, I know! I'm not pretending they are easy to achieve. It will take work, dedication, perhaps some difficult conversations with loved ones, and no small amount of pain. However, the results are worth it.

WHAT AILS US

According to the Centers for Disease Control and Prevention, 38 percent of all Americans are obese, and more than 70 percent are overweight or obese.[1] More than one in six children between the ages of six and nineteen are considered obese.

The United States used to be the fattest country in the world, but recently Mexico took over the top spot. Europe used to be much better than the US, but it's catching up. Today 50 percent of men and women in Europe are con-

---

1   "Obesity and Overweight," CDC National Center for Health Statistics, https://www.cdc.gov/nchs/fastats/obesity-overweight.htm

sidered overweight.[2] The World Health Organization reports that the percentage of obese people in the world nearly doubled between 1980 and 2008.

Obesity is now a global issue. In a recent study in the journal *Frontiers in Public Health*, researchers found 90 percent of men and 80 percent of women in the US and twenty-nine other developed countries have enough excess body fat to increase their risk of diabetes and heart disease.

When you consider the other health effects caused by obesity—in addition to diabetes and heart disease, cancer, high blood pressure, gallbladder disease, osteoarthritis, gout, and asthma are also associated with obesity—it becomes more frightening. These illnesses all cost money to treat.

Obesity also costs society. The heavier people are, the less work they can accomplish, and the more they call in sick to their jobs. One University of California, Davis obesity study in 2015 added up all the direct medical costs, lost-productivity costs from work absenteeism, short-term disability payments, and lost tax revenue and concluded that the lifetime cost of obesity is an average of $92,235 per person.[3]

---

2   "Data and statistics," World Health Organization Regional Office for Europe, http://www.euro.who.int/en/health-topics/noncommunicable-diseases/obesity/data-and-statistics

3   An in-depth look at the lifetime economic costs of obesity," The Brookings Institution, https://www.brookings.edu/events/an-in-depth-look-at-the-lifetime-economic-costs-of-obesity/

That's a staggering figure, and it becomes even more alarming when you consider that researchers predict half of all adults in our country will be obese by 2030.[4] If half of the population is ill or becoming ill with deadly, obesity-related diseases, how can the remaining half support them? Our health care system could collapse. This is an out-of-control train speeding down the tracks.

The annual medical cost of obesity in our country is nearly $150 billion, and if you're obese, you can expect to spend $1,429 more a year on medical expenses than someone with a normal weight.[5]

Obesity and diabetes, which I call diabesity, are closely associated. Diabetes affects thirty million adults and children in the US. More than eighty-four million Americans have prediabetes, meaning they are at risk of moving into type 2 diabetes, and 90 percent of those eighty-four million don't even know they are at risk. They only know they feel like crap. Every twenty-one seconds in this country, someone is diagnosed with diabetes. When that happens, they have a choice: they can either go on medicine or make a lifestyle change. When you have type 2 diabetes,

---

4   "F is for Fat: How Obesity Threatens America's Future 2011," Trust for America's Health, July 2011, http://healthyamericans.org/report/88/

5   "Adult Obesity Facts," Centers for Disease Control and Prevention, https://www.cdc.gov/obesity/data/adult.html

your health care costs are 2.3 times higher than someone who doesn't.[6]

It does not need to be this way. If we want to prevent diabesity from becoming a pandemic, we must learn discipline and take control of our lifestyles.

MY LIFE'S QUEST

Promoting healthy lifestyles and practices has been a central principle of my company from its inception. The idea for Steviva came to me in the late eighties after I met a man who had just returned from Paraguay. He had collected herbs and natural ingredients with the Guarani Indians, who live in jungles there. He had me taste a green paste from a vial. It was wonderfully sweet. He told me that it came from the stevia leaf and that it was twenty-five times sweeter than sugar but didn't have any calories. I was intrigued, to say the least.

I founded Steviva with the sole goal of getting those sweet components out of the stevia leaf and making a natural sweetener that food manufacturers could use instead of chemical sweeteners like aspartame or sucralose. I read

---

6   "The Staggering Costs of Diabetes," American Diabetes Association, http://www.diabetes.org/diabetes-basics/statistics/infographics/adv-staggering-cost-of-diabetes.html?referrer=https://www.google.com/

everything I could about diet and the effect of sugars on metabolic diseases.

I wanted a successful company, but part of my quest was personal. I was born in Milwaukee, Wisconsin, the land of cheese, beer, and bratwurst, and my family's diet was always rich in sugar and high-glycemic carbohydrates. High-glycemic carbohydrates are foods that spike your blood sugar and insulin. These are foods like table sugar, white rice, and bread and crackers made from refined flour. All cruciferous vegetables and nuts are considered low-glycemic foods because they have a slower, smaller effect on your blood sugar. All grains of any type should be avoided when following a ketogenic diet. They are complex carbohydrates that will throw you out of ketosis and flood your bloodstream and muscles with glucose. Diabetics often substitute fructose for sucrose (table sugar) because fructose has a lower glycemic index and won't cause a spike in their blood sugar. While fructose definitely has a lower glycemic impact, its dosage should be limited to under twenty grams per day. Fructose is metabolized by the liver, and if the liver gets overloaded, fructose will be stored as fat, which can accumulate around your middle and drive metabolic syndrome. *No bueno!*

I struggled with my weight after our family moved to a ranch in Colorado when I was thirteen. Part of the problem was that my parents fought a lot, so I turned to food to ease the stress. There were always sweet treats and sodas in the refrigerator.

As an adult struggling with his weight, I knew I had to cut sugars from my diet, so after I first tasted that green stevia paste, I made it my life's work to find a way to make a natural sweetener. At first, we could only sell stevia as a dietary supplement, but in 2008, the Food and Drug Administration approved stevia as a sweetener, and the company took off. Suddenly, food manufacturers came to us for our sweeteners.

Successful entrepreneurs find the things that make them burn with passion. For me, it was stevia. I not only wanted a successful company, but I wanted a company that changed people's lives, including Steviva's own employees.

Steviva is a small, agile company with a collaborative environment. Every employee has a voice in how the company is run. We have raised-bed gardens people use to grow their own food. We have a yoga studio and a climbing wall. We have chickens, and employees can collect eggs. We emphasize health and fitness at company events, and almost everybody who works here ends up on a ketogenic diet. It's amazing.

Most importantly, our employees understand the stewardship of the land and animals and the role we all play in the ecosystem we live and work in. I wanted a company that promoted healthy lifestyles and helped people feel more alive. I think we achieve this, but this process, like the process of getting fit and reaching a healthy weight, needs to be a long-term commitment.

Are you ready to make one?

FIRST STEPS

In this book, I'll show you the steps I have taken on my quest to lose weight and get fit. For now, here are some things to keep in mind:

- Set a goal for how much weight you want to lose and which parts of your lifestyle you want to change. Write it down.
- If you want to lose weight, do it slowly and methodically. Shoot for losing one to two pounds a week. Losing weight any faster leaves you with saggy skin, and if you do it too fast, you're more likely to gain it back. Lose weight with a combination of diet and exercise.
- Learn how sugar and high-glycemic carbohydrates, like crackers, cereals, and bread, affect you and how switching to a ketogenic diet rich in healthy fats, including foods like salmon, tuna, avocados, and nuts, will benefit you.

- Trust the process. I'm fifty-seven years old, and I started down this path when I was fifty-six. I lost thirty-five pounds in one year. If I can do it, anyone can. I love pizza, beer, cake, and ice cream as much as the next person, but I've cut it from my diet. Find the discipline and enlist a strong support group.
- Pay it forward. One reason I wrote this book is that I learned at a young age that knowledge and good fortune should be shared. If you read this book, adopt a ketogenic lifestyle, and enjoy dramatic changes in your weight, health, and mental capacity, *promise to pay it forward* by teaching someone else what you've learned.

By the end of this book, you will understand how your body functions metabolically. You'll have the confidence to control your weight, diet, and health. You may even see improvements in your short- and long-term memory and overall cognitive abilities. I know I did. You'll feel in control of your machine.

You'll also understand how the ketogenic diet affects brain chemistry, and how your body can burn ketone bodies rather than sugar and carbohydrates. You'll learn how to identify and avoid the hidden sugars in processed food that can take you out of ketosis, which is a metabolic state in which you burn ketones from fat rather than blood glucose from sugar and carbohydrates. You'll save money when you shop. I'll also set you up with meal plans and recipes so you can hit the ground running. So let's begin!

Part I

GOING KETO

Chapter 1

———

YO-YO WEIGHT

Before going keto, I experimented with a lot of different diets. One was the cabbage soup diet.[1] A heart surgeon developed it for his patients to eat prior to heart surgery. You eat nothing but cabbage soup for seven days straight.

It was fantastic for the first couple of days. The soup is delicious. The weight melts off. I lost ten pounds the first week. The problem was, after a week, I got so sick of the soup I couldn't stomach it any longer. This made the diet unsustainable. Who wants to eat cabbage soup for the rest of his life? So I quit—and regained all the weight I'd lost.

I also tried the master cleanse lemonade diet. Each day, I drank six to twelve glasses of lemonade made from fresh lemons, maple syrup, and cayenne pepper. That's it. Nothing but lemonade for ten days straight. I also lost

---

1   "The Cabbage Soup Diet," WebMD, https://www.webmd.com/diet/a-z/cabbage-soup-diet

weight on this diet, but when I went back to my regular diet, I gained back all the weight I'd lost and then some.

The problem with these diets is that your body goes into a state of unhealthy starvation and, as a result, conserves energy in your fat cells. Once your body has experienced unhealthy starvation, your metabolism is altered, and your body goes into a mode of extreme conservation, preparing itself for a life of starvation. When you eat normally again, your body remains in this state and converts all the fats, sugars, and carbohydrates into the fat stores it thinks you'll need during the next bout of unhealthy starvation. Consequently, you don't burn as many carbohydrates, and you get fatter around the middle.

The problem is, although these diets can help you lose weight in the near term, you haven't made a lifestyle change that makes the diet and the weight loss sustainable and long lasting. Remember, weight loss is 80 percent diet and 20 percent exercise, and the most successful approach incorporates changes to both over a long period.[2] The faster you lose weight, the more likely you are to gain it back. The more you rely on diet alone, the less likely you are to succeed.

---

2   Aaron E. Carroll, June 15, 2015, "To Lose Weight, Eating Less is Far More Important Than Exercising More," *New York Times*, https://www.nytimes.com/2015/06/16/upshot/to-lose-weight-eating-less-is-far-more-important-than-exercising-more.html

Just as you have a physical reaction to normal eating after an unhealthy starvation diet, you can also experience an emotional reaction. Your food cravings, for example, will become acute, and you will crave sugar or high-glycemic carbohydrates.

A lot of those food cravings are food addictions. When you look at how your brain reacts when it eats sugar, it's almost identical to the brain's reaction to cocaine, which everyone knows is addictive. The same hormones and dopamine triggered by cocaine can be triggered by certain foods. When you come off ten days of cabbage soup, and you're ten pounds lighter, you feel this great freedom to reward yourself with your favorite foods. Once you indulge in sugar and high-glycemic carbohydrates, it's like doing a line of cocaine. You throw yourself back into addictive behavior.

Dropping out of a diet and indulging your food addictions backfires and brings on self-loathing and crippling self-esteem issues. When that weight comes back and then goes even higher than before you started the diet, it brings with it a level of unhealthy shame. How do you deal with the shame? You eat more of your comfort foods. It's a terrible cycle, but it's very real for many people.

This cycle of weight loss, weight gain, and resorting to sugary, high-glycemic foods feeds a toxic mindset. You can't stop your late-night eating. You can't stop snacking. This toxic mindset is the most destructive aspect of yo-yo dieting.

LEVERAGING PAIN AND SUFFERING FOR SUCCESS

Diets deliver temporary results. There isn't a single diet out there that will deliver lasting results and increase your health and longevity. The only way to achieve that is through permanent lifestyle changes.

To make permanent lifestyle changes, you need persistence, commitment, and discipline. Of these three, discipline is the overarching need. The only way to achieve that is to leverage your emotional and physical pain.

When a child sticks his finger in a flame, and it hurts, they learn not to play with fire. You must approach your weight and your eating habits with the same principle. If you can associate pain with eating sugars or high-glycemic carbohydrates, you can develop the discipline you need to eat better and exercise.

I'm talking about the physical pain you feel when your clothes don't fit, when your belt cuts into your stomach, and when your knees ache because you carry around an extra thirty pounds of fat. It's the suffering you feel climbing out of your car or bending over to tie your shoes. It's the pain of not being able to hike because you can't keep up and you can't catch your breath.

I'm talking about the emotional suffering you feel when you need a seat belt extender on an airplane. People say they don't judge overweight people, but they do, and you feel ashamed. You tell yourself you don't care what other people think, but you do. When people don't want to sit next to you on a plane, you feel pain. It's the pain and suffering of being judged. It's the pain of your own self-loathing.

Leverage that pain and suffering.

When you sit down in front of a pizza, think about the physical or emotional discomfort your weight makes you feel. Now associate that pain with the pizza in front of you. Imagine how that pizza will only increase your pain. At that very moment, understand that you can do something about that pain by not eating a slice of pizza. Ask yourself, "Do I want to trade two minutes of pleasure eating a piece of pizza for two days of feeling discouraged and disappointed in myself?"

I don't think you do.

You must take responsibility for the shape you're in. You allowed it to happen, and now it's up to you to do something about it. The only way to change things is to make a 100 percent commitment to discipline and lifestyle change. Become sensitive to your pain and tie negative habits to that pain. When you acknowledge your pain, you can create better habits.

ATTITUDES AND HABITS SHAPED BY ENVIRONMENT

Your environment can play a key role in shaping your attitudes about food and lifestyle. Your environment can foster healthy attitudes, but it can also instill bad habits, food addictions, and emotional dysfunction.

My life is a good example. I grew up in a state of poverty. My dad studied engineering at the University of Colorado, and we never had much money. We ate a lot of spaghetti because you can buy a box of spaghetti for a buck and feed a family on five bucks. Spaghetti and a lot of the other foods we ate are very cheap and very starchy. I had a lot of fluctuations in my weight as a result.

When I was older, my dad started a construction firm and enjoyed some financial success. We moved to a ranch, and I developed some different attitudes toward food.

I did everything on that ranch. I branded the cattle, cut their horns, castrated bulls, repaired fences. In the winter before school, I broke the creek ice so the cattle could get water. I hauled out bales of hay to feed them. This was the catalyst for my interest in health and nutrition. I saw how our food and the planet are interconnected. Taking care of animals and the land gave me a deeper appreciation of where our food comes from. You respect the animal that's given its life for your food. You respect the vegetables that have emerged from the earth.

A cornerstone of the ketogenic lifestyle is refraining from mindless eating while being mindful of where our food comes from and what we put in our bodies. This is why, at Steviva, we maintain nine raised vegetable gardens and a flock of egg-laying chickens. People can go out to the garden and pick greens for their lunchtime salad. They collect eggs to cook. We share the food and the work to raise it.

Raising food or being cognizant of where it comes from is part of the long-term lifestyle changes that help you lose weight and get healthier. Waiting for that tomato to ripen in the garden slows down your thinking, teaches you patience, and makes you that much more appreciative of the delicious food you will enjoy when that tomato turns red. If I've learned anything in the last year, it's that there are no quick fixes. You can't stabilize your weight and get fit overnight. It's a lifelong journey. You must be able to make a lifelong commitment to health and fitness.

There are few guarantees in life. However, if you promise

to make a change and you keep that promise, I guarantee you'll feel better. You'll have higher self-esteem. It will be the greatest expression of love and acceptance you can give yourself.

LET'S GET STARTED

If you're ready to start this journey, buy yourself a journal. You can't have a successful journey without leaving a trail of where you've been. Make it a nice journal, not a crappy notebook, because what you write in it will have great sacred value and should be treated with respect.

Write down your goals and record all your progress toward them. Tell others about your goals—that makes them real and helps you keep your sights on them.

Part of the goal-setting process is to understand why you have set that goal. Without understanding your why, you'll never advance to your how. Why do you want to lose that weight? Why are you committing to this lifestyle change?

It might be you want to lose weight so you can be more active, or maybe you want to attract the man or woman you've always dreamt of being with. You might want to free yourself from the shame of being obese. You might have a hundred whys. Whatever the number, write down your reasons for making this lifestyle change. If you fill up your journal, go buy another one. The more whys you have, the more you'll be able to engage the how.

Create a journal that reflects what is important to you. Here are some things you should consider including:

- Weight: Jump on the scale first thing in the morning. A lot of people think you shouldn't weigh yourself every day because they think it's discouraging. I think that's bullshit. Recording your data for each day will help you get a clearer picture of your patterns.
- A "before" picture of yourself: Photograph yourself without any clothes on and add it to your journal. Take self-portraits each week and file them in the proper location in your journal so you can see the progress you make.
- Diet: What you ate that day and when you ate it. Include calories consumed as well as sugar and fat content if you have that information.
- Beverages: Keep track of how much you drank, from coffee and water to wine.
- Sleep: Take note of how many hours you slept and how restful your sleep was. Include naps.
- Exercise: I have friends who record a lot of details on their workouts, from how many miles they run to how many steps they take. They keep track of how long it takes them to complete a set workout, and some even keep track of their average heart rate and how

many calories they burn. Take note of how you felt during exercise.

- Emotions: How are you feeling? Make a note of what's bothering you or what excites you.
- More measurements: Get kits from the pharmacy to measure your blood sugar and ketone levels. These measurements help you ensure you remain in ketosis—or alert you to make adjustments in your diet.

Morning is the best time to write in your journal. Morning is when you can create the map for the rest of your day and reflect on the previous day. When I get up, I record my weight and reflect on it. Did it go up or down? Why did it go down? Did I drink more fluids during the day? Did I eat after 6 p.m.? Did I snack during the day? In Chapter 4, I'll talk more about my morning "Hour of Power," which is when I use exercise, meditation, reflection, and a strong dose of Bulletproof Coffee to set the tone for my day.

The goal of keeping a journal is not to drive yourself crazy with statistics. The goal is to be engaged and pay close attention to your behavior. This is a lifestyle change, not a casual experiment, so you need to remain focused on your goals and your habits to ensure you stay on track. Once you see results, it creates a level of excitement within you.

PAY IT FORWARD

Once I saw the results of this ketogenic lifestyle, I felt compelled to share it—with my friends, my customers, with the world. It's one reason I wrote this book. Paying it forward is part of the price of achievement. You are obligated to empower others. Tell them about your journey and show them how they can succeed, too.

Before I started, I couldn't do ten pushups. I was thirty-five pounds overweight, and my blood pressure was dangerously high. I believe I would be dead today if I hadn't started on this journey, and I feel I must share my story with the world or with anyone who will listen. If I can impact just one other person's life, that will be a huge success for me.

Many of my customers have shared their stories about adopting a ketogenic lifestyle. One customer, Jody Bailey, said she started her ketogenic lifestyle because she was overweight and her doctor recommended a high-protein, high-fat diet.

"People around me thought I was crazy," Jody wrote to me recently. "But sugar made me fat, and my body's metabolism did not work with sugar, and artificial sweeteners were killing me. I went through a period where I suffered palpitations and learned that aspartame was causing it. Three days after I stopped using it, the palpitations went away. I've been ketogenic ever since."

Jody, like many others, limits her high-glycemic carbohydrates. It was difficult for her to give up bread, but she has. "When I stick to the diet," Jody told me, "I find I feel better and have a lot more energy; and yes, I lost weight too."

Jody's not alone. Cheryl Van Tessier, a public relations executive, ate a diet rich in "healthy" grains and fruit before slowly reducing carbs and sugars and increasing healthy fats.

"Since incorporating these simple but powerful changes into my diet, I have noticed fewer cravings—hunger no longer runs my life—less bloating, and even clearer skin and fewer headaches, both of which I've battled for years," Cheryl told me. "Additionally, people I haven't seen in a while have started commenting on how much weight I have lost. My family has noticed too and has even begun watching their own sugar intake. My teenage children have even started asking me not to bring sugary treats into the house—something I never thought I'd hear!"

John Shattuck, a senior buyer for Nellson LLC, the only full-service bar and powder nutrition provider in North America, adopted a ketogenic diet after years of following a diet free of sugar, soy, gluten, and many types of dairy. Although his "very clean" diet kept him thin, increased his energy levels, and eliminated pesky sinus issues, he went off the diet in his late twenties and watched as his weight climbed from 140 pounds to 217.

"My food choices were out of control, and weight was going up as my energy and motivation for life were falling through the floor," John told me one day when I was finishing up this book. "I would wake up tired and lethargic, go through the day this way, and have little energy to do much in the evening. I was only thirty years old."

About this time—the summer of 2017—John and I were both attending the same conference, and he asked me about a ketogenic diet.

"Our conversation around keto and what you had found it did for you was inspiring," John said.

He also started watching YouTube videos by a guy named Jason Wittrock, an athlete who follows a ketogenic diet. John decided to change his lifestyle.

"Since beginning this lifestyle back in July 2017, my energy has tripled. I feel like I am twenty-one again. I've shed 12 percent of my bodyweight since changing to keto, and I've had no real blood sugar or mood issues."

John feels the ketogenic diet has "opened up a new ability to live life more fully."

"With better rest, more energy, and a positive attitude, there is not much that can stop good things from happening," he said. "I sincerely thank you for the inspiration you provided. It was probably not intentional, but our conversation came at the perfect time in my journey."

Success stories like these are encouraging, and I hope yours will be, too.

IT'S UP TO YOU

Adopting a ketogenic lifestyle is a big step. It's not for people who are playing around. You must be committed to success.

If you're not committed, then this book isn't for you. Give it away or return it. Maybe the ketogenic lifestyle isn't for you. Perhaps there isn't enough pain associated with your health to convince you to make a change. If you're happy eating pizza and drinking beer a couple of nights a week, if you're not upset about being fifty pounds overweight, then keep doing what you're doing. When the student is ready, the teacher will appear.

It's up to you to make the commitment, hold yourself accountable, and do the work. If you don't, you won't succeed. That's OK, because more than half of the US population is stuck, too. You will just be part of that 70 percent of the population that's overweight or obese and facing an increased risk of diabetes and other diseases.

Take a good look at yourself in the mirror and ask, "Do I want to be ordinary, or do I want to be extraordinary?" If you're happy being in the 70 percent that's overweight, fine. If you're comfortable with that, then ask yourself, "Why did I buy this book?"

However, if you commit and keep a journal of your journey and surround yourself with supportive people, the results can be astonishing. When you look back a year in your journal, you'll see how different you have become. You won't recognize yourself. That's how powerful this is. I've seen it—in myself and in dozens and dozens of people I know.

When you make the commitment, build a plan, work your plan, and journal daily, you will be successful. There is no way you can't be.

Chapter 2

THE KETOGENIC DIET

People have followed ketogenic diets since 500 BC, when the ancient Greeks used fasting and high-fat, low-carbohydrate diets to help patients suffering from periodic seizures. The term "ketogenic diet" was coined in the 1920s when doctors at the Mayo Clinic also used a diet rich in fat and low in carbohydrates to treat epileptics.[1]

According to the Charlie Foundation for Ketogenic Therapies, which provides diet therapies and information for epileptics and others suffering neurological disorders, the diet reduced seizures in up to 80 percent of patients diagnosed with epilepsy. In 2006 the Charlie Foundation commissioned a panel of neurologists and dietitians with

---

[1] "The Ketogenic Diet," The Charlie Foundation, https://www.charliefoundation.org/explore-ketogenic-diet/explore-1/introducing-the-diet

expertise in using the ketogenic diet to create a consensus statement in support of the clinical management of the ketogenic diet and when it should be considered. Children are especially good candidates for the diet, owing to their reliance on adults for nourishment and to the nature of a young developing brain.

Epilepsy affects fifty million people worldwide[2] and is diagnosed simply by the occurrence of two or more unprovoked seizures. Seizures occur when nerve cells signal incorrectly and can result in strange sensations, emotions, behavior, convulsions, or a loss of consciousness. There are many causes for epilepsy, including illness, brain injury, abnormal brain development, and genetic conditions. Epilepsy is more common in young children and in the elderly.

Thirty percent of people who have epilepsy do not respond to antiseizure medications. According to a 2010 study in the *New England Journal of Medicine*,[3] people who developed childhood epilepsy had a substantially higher death rate if their seizures were not controlled over a five-year period. Around the same time that doctors at the Mayo Clinic started using a ketogenic diet to treat epileptics, endocrinologist Rollin Woodyatt discovered

---

2   "Epilepsy," World Health Organization, http://www.who.int/mediacentre/factsheets/fs999/en/

3   "Long-Term Mortality in Childhood-Onset Epilepsy," The New England Journal of Medicine, December 23, 2010, http://www.nejm.org/doi/full/10.1056/NEJMoa0911610

water-soluble compounds in our bodies he called "ketone bodies." The liver makes ketones from fats when there is insufficient sugar or carbohydrates to supply energy—such as with people who follow a fat-rich, protein-rich, and carbohydrate-restricted diet. Woodyatt found that when the body is starved of sugar, it burns ketones for energy. Burning ketones is a more efficient way of producing energy. It delivers a steadier, more reliable burn than sugar or simple carbohydrates. Simple carbs with one sugar molecule (fructose, glucose, and galactose) are called monosaccharides, while those with two sugar molecules (sucrose, maltose, and lactose) are known as disaccharides. Simple sugars are also recognized as processed and refined sugars as well as complex carbohydrates. Complex carbohydrates are made up of sugar molecules that are strung together in long, complex chains. Complex carbohydrates are found in foods such as peas, beans, whole grains, and vegetables. Both simple and complex carbohydrates are turned to glucose (blood sugar) in the body and can take you out of a ketogenic state. This forces the body to burn glycogen. Glycogen is made up of many glucose molecules and is stored in our muscles and liver for when the body needs a quick boost of energy and isn't getting glucose from food. Burning glycogen can cause spikes in your blood sugar and insulin levels.

MELTING AWAY FAT

A ketogenic diet changes the way your body uses energy. By reducing your sugar and carbohydrates, your body goes into a state of starvation for those energy sources and looks elsewhere for energy. It finds it in the subcutaneous fat areas of your body—such as the fatty areas of your stomach—and pulls glycogen from the fat.[4] The liver metabolizes these glycogens and converts them to ketone bodies. You burn the ketone bodies for energy, and your fat stores melt away.

That's how the diet helps you lose weight—by burning up the glycogen stored in the fat around your belly and other places you don't want it. Once your glycogen stores run out, and your liver produces more ketones, your body shifts from burning glycogen to burning ketones. That means you're in a state of ketosis. When it's tuned up, your body produces a deep, rich, and almost endless supply of ketones to burn.

Many people associate the ketogenic diet with the Atkins diet. The Atkins diet put more emphasis on reduced carbohydrate consumption instead of the high fats of the ketogenic diet, but both approaches have the same effect:

---

4   "Ketones," Diabetes Education Online, The University of California, San Francsico, https://dtc.ucsf.edu/types-of-diabetes/type2/understanding-type-2-diabetes/how-the-body-processes-sugar/ketones/

each will put you in a ketogenic state in which you burn energy from ketones rather than glycogen.

A diet rich in healthy fats forces your liver to produce ketones faster than a high-protein diet. The fats you eat from things like salmon, tuna, grass-fed beef, nuts, olives, eggs, seeds, and avocados will help keep you in ketosis. Healthy fats include:

- Polyunsaturated fats, such as omega-3 and omega-6 fatty acids, which are essential fatty acids because our bodies don't produce them and we must get them from food. Polyunsaturated fats from certain nuts, seeds, fish, and vegetable oils can lower total cholesterol levels.
- Monosaturated fats, like those found in avocados, olive oil, canola oil, and peanut oil, and many nuts and seeds.

We have been lied to. We have been told that fats are bad. Many people still believe that old-school way of thinking. The truth is, some fats are good for you. Our bodies need fats. Fat is necessary for you to lose weight. But it's important to know which fats are good and which ones you should avoid.

By and large, the fats to avoid are trans fats and saturated fats. These fats are often found in packaged foods like margarine, bake mixes, and heavily processed foods. These fats will raise LDL (bad cholesterol) and lower your HDL (good cholesterol). The reason these fats are so unhealthy is because most of them have undergone hydrogenation.

Hydrogenation is a chemical process that food manufacturers use to keep the fat in packaged food from going rancid. These trans fats are hard to catch on food labels because the law allows the food manufacturers to label them as zero grams of trans fat if the product contains less than 0.5 grams. This is such bullshit.

Saturated fat found naturally in animal and plant sources is not villainous, but the trans fats found in margarine, shortening, and partially hydrogenated vegetable oils used in low-quality products are.

Unsaturated fats such as omega-3, omega-6, oleic acid, and linoleic acids are considered good fats. Adding copious servings of these into your diet can actually help you lose weight and keep you satiated. Essential, fat-soluble vitamins A, D, E, and K all require fat so that they can be absorbed into the body. Without fat, you will not be getting any of these essential vitamins. Foods high in unsaturated fats, such as avocado, can actually keep you feeling full longer because they can take a longer time to digest. These good fats will keep you in a ketogenic state.

A ketogenic diet is 70 percent healthy fat, 20 percent protein, and 10 percent carbohydrates, with the carbohydrates primarily coming from cruciferous vegetables, such as broccoli, cauliflower, kale, spinach, and other plants that grow above the ground. If it grows below the ground, chances are it is high glycemic and will take you out of ketosis.

My first experience with a ketogenic diet was through the Atkins diet. Dr. Atkins brought the diet out from being a clinical treatment for epilepsy, strokes, and heart disease to being a popular way to lose weight and get fit. The success of the diet was a springboard for other researchers, like Dr. Dom D'Agostino of the University of South Florida, to explore the science behind the diet. Dr. D'Agostino, a powerlifter and weight trainer, studies the benefits ketone bodies can have for high-performance athletes.

That research has gone a long way toward dispelling some of the myths that have been perpetuated by the consumer food industry, which for years has told us that sugar gives us energy, fat makes you fat, and carbohydrates power your body. None of that is true, and now researchers like Dr. D'Agostino explore healthier alternatives for improving performance through ketogenic diets.

THE HEALTH BENEFITS OF KETOGENICS

Ketogenics is not just a great way to lose weight. It has a

wealth of additional benefits. It fights diabetes, cardio-vascular problems, cancer, and brain degeneration.

Diabetes is a disease that affects how your body deals with glucose in your blood. Glucose is a kind of sugar that comes from the food you eat, but you need insulin, a hormone made by your pancreas, to convert food to glucose. People with type 2 diabetes cannot utilize insulin the way they should, and this causes a buildup of sugar in your blood.

According to the Centers for Disease Control and Prevention, about twenty-nine million people in the US have type 2 diabetes, and eighty-six million have prediabetes, which means their blood glucose is not normal but not high enough to be classified as type 2 diabetes. Unless these prediabetics lose weight and get some exercise, the CDC predicts 15 to 30 percent of that eighty-six million will develop type 2 diabetes within five years. That means millions of people face the serious health consequences of diabetes, including vision loss, heart disease, stroke, kidney failure, amputation of toes, feet, or legs, and premature death, the CDC says.[5]

But according to researchers at the Harvard School of

---

5   "Prevent Complications," The Centers for Disease Control, https://www.cdc.gov/diabetes/managing/problems.html

Public Health, if you can drop 7 to 10 percent of your body weight, you can cut the risk of type 2 diabetes in half.[6]

One of the first studies on how a ketogenic diet can affect diabetes was conducted at Duke University in 2005.[7] Twenty-one overweight patients were put on a ketogenic diet for sixteen weeks, and each person lost an average of twenty pounds.

The greatest impact, however, was on blood glucose levels. Those decreased an average of 17 percent, and the average amount of fat in the blood decreased 41.6 percent. Most of the subjects could discontinue their diabetes medication after they switched to a ketogenic diet.

There is also evidence that decreasing a person's body fat through a ketogenic diet can help forestall cardiovascular diseases. Researchers in Switzerland, for example, put mice on a high-fat, moderate-protein, low-carbohydrate diet and lowered the mice's body fat by more than 30 percent. Obesity and high body fat are linked to heart disease. According to the *Journal of the American College*

6   "Obesity: Can we stop the epidemic?", *Harvard Public Health*, Harvard School of Public Health, https://www.hsph.harvard.edu/magazine/magazine_article/obesity/

7   "A low-carbohydrate, ketogenic diet to treat Type 2 diabetes," Nutrition and Metabolism, Dec. 1, 2005, https://www.ncbi.nlm.nih.gov/pmc/articles/PMC1325029/

of Cardiology, belly fat, in particular, increases the risk of heart disease.[8]

FIGHTING CANCER AND DEMENTIA

A ketogenic diet won't cure cancer, but it can help prevent cancer from getting a toehold in your body.

Rogue cancer cells are found even in healthy people, and those cells thrive on glucose. That's why, when doctors want to see how bad your cancer is, they inject you with glucose laced with a radioactive isotope. Cancer cells use glucose faster than normal cells, so the radioactive isotope in the glucose will reveal any high concentration of cancer cells in your body. Every time you eat sugar or take in an overabundance of glucose, you feed those cancer cells. When your diet is rich in fats and proteins, you starve those cancer cells.

When you go into a state of ketosis and burn ketones for energy, cancer cells can't adapt. They rely on glucose and can't survive in a body that's in a state of ketosis. The National Institutes of Health has written a report on how cancer cells can't metabolize ketones and why a keto-

---

8   "Study Shows More Reasons Why Belly Fat is Dangerous for the Heart," American
     College of Cardiology, http://www.acc.org/about-acc/press-releases/2016/09/26/15/13/
     study-shows-more-reasons-why-belly-fat-is-dangerous-for-the-heart

genic diet might be an alternative therapy for treating malignant tumors.

According to Shelly Fan, writing in 2013 for *Scientific American* as a PhD candidate in neuroscience at the University of British Columbia, animal studies and clinical trials suggest a ketogenic diet can be used to treat certain neurodegenerative diseases, sleep disorder, bipolar disorder, autism, and brain cancer.

One of the latest findings is that a ketogenic diet, along with intermittent fasting, can prevent brain degeneration and diseases like Alzheimer's and dementia.[9] These diseases are now increasingly referred to as type 3 diabetes because of the role sugar and carbohydrates play in the brain chemistry that results in plaque buildup in the brain.

Your brain sits in a fluid bath where peptides, a chain of amino acids similar to but smaller than proteins, hook up with the receptors in your brain. That's how brain function works. When you burn these peptides, it leaves behind a waste product—think of it as an ash left behind after a fire goes out—that needs to be swept out of the brain. A scientific study of mouse brains showed how ours handle this buildup of waste. While we are in ketosis or a fasted state, our circulatory system rapidly pumps fluid along

---

9   "Ketogenic Diets and Alzheimer's Disease," *Food Science and Human Wellness*, Vol. 6, Issue 1, https://www.sciencedirect.com/science/article/pii/S2213453016301355

the outside of blood vessels surrounding our brain, literally flushing this waste away. These results, reported in *Science Translational Medicine*, showed how neurodegenerative diseases like dementia and Alzheimer's develop and might be treated.

Cerebrospinal fluid flows along the outside of blood vessels, carried through a network of pipe-like protein structures. The fluid picks up waste that accumulates between cells, then drains out through major veins. This flushing action is blocked when high amounts of glucose are present in the blood.

Aside from cerebrospinal fluid flushing, there are many different ways your body gets rid of accumulated waste and toxins. One biological process is known as autophagy.

The term "autophagy" means "self-eating," and refers to the processes by which your body cleans out various debris, including toxins, and recycles damaged cell components.

Autophagy is necessary to keep the body clean and free from rogue cells. The process occurs in all cells in the body. But when you eat too much sugar or high-glycemic carbohydrates, your brain fails to flush out these discarded materials, and plaque can build up. Amyloidal plaque, one byproduct, leads to Alzheimer's, and Lewy body plaque, another byproduct, leads to dementia. These plaques coat your brain and prevent proper brain function. The role sugar plays in that process is one reason why researchers have referred to these associated brain diseases as type 3 diabetes.

I believe the rates of dementia and Alzheimer's in this country are rising because of the sugar and high-glycemic carbohydrates people consume.

My father may have been an example. All his life, he loved sweets. He ate a lot of ice cream and donuts—I guess those were his comfort foods. Five years before he died, he developed dementia and was unable to care for himself or carry on conversations. He also developed prostate cancer, and toward the end of his life, he had a complete loss of appetite and stopped eating. I was with him at that time, and I think his body was starved of sugar and carbohydrates and that he began burning ketone bodies. His breath developed a sweet odor with a hint of acetone, a sign he was in ketosis.

In the last month of his life, before cancer killed him, his comprehension and clarity returned. He was more lucid than he had been in years. My theory is that his diet put him in ketosis, improved his brain autophagy, and flushed away plaque from his brain.

SUGAR IS THE ENEMY

Another myth you often hear is that the brain functions best on glucose. That is not necessarily true. Some parts of some brain cells can only burn glucose, but our bodies, through ketosis, can turn protein into glucose through a process known as gluconeogenesis. This means that, while there are essential requirements for both fat and protein, we can live quite happily while consuming no carbohydrates at all.

While the body is in a nutritional ketogenic state, ketones serve as an alternative energy source to maintain normal brain cell metabolism. In fact, beta-hydroxybutyric acid, a key ketone, has been shown to be a more efficient fuel than glucose, providing more energy per unit of oxygen used.

A ketogenic diet also increases the number of mitochondria, the power sources in our brain cells. According to Shelly Fan in *Scientific American*, a recent study found "enhanced expression of genes encoding for mitochondrial enzymes and energy metabolism in the hippocampus, a part of the brain important for learning and memory." Fan noted how hippocampal cells frequently "degenerate in age-related brain diseases, leading to cognitive dysfunction and memory loss. With increased energy reserve, neurons may be able to ward off disease stressors that would usually exhaust and kill the cell." Shazam!

Mitochondria are the batteries in each cell. They are the

tiny rod-like structures that produce the energy that cells run on and that bodies need to survive. They run on ketone bodies, so when you produce more ketone bodies, those mitochondria in your brain cells increase the amount of energy available to the brain.

Once you're in a state of ketosis, something as simple as eating a teaspoon of ice cream can throw you out of it. The sugar in the ice cream forces the body to switch from burning ketones to burning glycogen again, and you will continue burning it until it's all gone. This could take a few hours, or it could take a few days. If you eat too much sugar, your body will convert any glycogen you don't burn into fat.

Another problem with the sudden influx of sugar is the effect it has on the bacteria in your gut. There are about three hundred to five hundred different types of bacteria in your gut, and some of it thrives on glucose. The more glucose there is, the more some types of bacteria will grow. One of those is candida, a yeast that can grow out of control when there is an abundance of glucose for it to feed on. The result is an intense craving for more sugar (to feed this billowing cloud of candida), as well as bloating, depression, anxiety, digestive issues, and an inability to think clearly. You might also experience itchy skin and, since your gut is responsible for 90 percent of your immune system, a weakened immune system.

As you can see, sugar is not just an enemy of your waistline. It can have a big impact on your digestive system as well as your brain function.

WHAT TO EXPECT WHEN YOU GO KETO

"Going keto" brings terrific health benefits, but making the transition from a sugar- and carbohydrate-laden diet to a ketogenic diet is challenging. You may feel the pain of withdrawal when you cut sugar and carbs. That's because sugar, as I mentioned earlier, activates the same area of the brain as cocaine or heroin. Sugar intake also triggers the release of dopamine—that feel-good hormone—and when you lose that, you may experience some depression and lethargy. You also may experience mood swings and irritability as your body recalibrates from burning sugar and high-glycemic carbs to burning ketones.

The transition, also called the "keto flu," can last up to thirty days. Some people get through it in two to seven days. This is when the body breaks down the fatty acids in your subcutaneous fats and then converts it over to ketones for fuel.

However long the transition takes, there are ways to mitigate the effects. Over-the-counter ketone salts, or exogenous ketones, can help ease the irritability and get you into ketosis faster.

You also need to make sure you remain hydrated. A lot of times, you feel hungry when in fact you are thirsty. Also, your body will use water to metabolize fats into ketone bodies, so the more water you drink, the more calories you'll burn and the more support you'll give your liver as it cranks up the effort to produce ketone bodies.

THE BENEFITS OF FASTING

Although fasting is not a good weight-loss tool, many medical experts believe fasting can help you get rid of the toxins in the body. Advocates say fasting stimulates the cellular-cleansing process of autophagy, recycling the cellular debris that many experts say is responsible for some of the effects of aging. Fasting ensures you are in a state of ketosis and burning fat, which is where the body stores environmental toxins. Fasting isn't a good idea if you have liver or kidney problems or are on certain types of medication.

I do what's called a "black fast," which means no food or water for two days, as well as no contact with water during that time. That's right—no showers, no teeth brushing. This type of fast is the most enlightening for me. I've had moments of great clarity during a black fast. The fast also kicked my fat burning into high gear and gave me confidence I could handle anything. It taught me better control over my hunger.

To take your mind off food and drink, go for walks, rest, reflect, or binge on Netflix. Resisting food and drink is your way of taking control and doing something healthy for your body and mind. After one fast, I took an online test through Lumosity.com and found my brain function had increased by 30 percent.

Another technique is called "intermittent fasting," which is when you only eat during a six-hour period of the day and fast the remaining eighteen hours. You can accomplish this by eating your last meal of the day at 7 p.m. and waiting till noon the next day to eat your next meal. From 12 p.m. to 7 p.m., eat as you normally would, staying with the ketogenic menu. This is another way to get your body accustomed to burning fat rather than sugar or carbs.

Another option is to fast for one or two days every three months. You need to work up to a fast like this, however, because it can be a struggle at first. However, with that struggle come beautiful lessons and growth.

Going keto means changing how you eat and how you burn energy. Exercise will help you in the transition period by assisting in burning off all the glycogen you have stored. You should continue to exercise when you're in ketosis.

Remember, this is a marathon, not a sprint. This is a lifestyle change. It's a lifelong commitment.

If you're with me, read on.

Part II

———

KNOW THY LABEL

Chapter 3

———

SO MUCH SUGAR

When I was a kid, I played football and baseball. I exercised frequently, but my weight still went up and down. I would work out like crazy, go on short-term diets, and lose weight. The second I went off the diet, however, the weight would come right back.

I needed a lifestyle change. Diets, I learned, are temporary; lifestyle changes are permanent.

I've found that if you try to lose weight and get fit, 20 percent of your success will come from exercise and the remaining 80 percent will come from modifying your diet. Exercise can be anything you enjoy doing—going for a run or a walk, riding a bike, or going to the gym. Movement exercises like yoga, tai chi, or martial arts can also be part of the equation. I also make meditation part of my routine.

As for diet, I've had the best success with a ketogenic diet, and a key element of that approach is cutting out the culprit that causes so many health problems in society today: sugar.

MY EXPERIENCE WITH SUGAR

When I realized a few years ago that exercising and diets weren't a permanent solution to my fluctuating weight, I used a process of elimination to discover that sugar was my main nemesis.

Growing up, I loved sugar. Everyone in my family did. We always had ice cream in the freezer, and as I mentioned in the introduction, I turned to food, particularly ice cream, when I was a boy to manage the stress of my parents fighting.

By the time I got to college, I ate sugar all day, every day. I believed that sugar gave you energy, so I'd consume it often and in quantity.

Have you heard of Zingers? These are Twinkies covered and filled with icing, and my favorites were the ones with coconut shavings and raspberry jam. My breakfast consisted of two packs of Hostess Zingers, chased with chocolate milk.

At midday, I'd start slamming M&M-stacked Pepsis. I

would dump a bag of M&M's into the Pepsi and let them dissolve a little before I started drinking it. About three-quarters of the way through the Pepsi, I'd reach this rich chocolate-Pepsi-flavored syrup containing whatever whole M&M's hadn't dissolved. A crunchy soft drink!

All this put me on a blood sugar rollercoaster. I'd get an immediate burst of energy from the sugar, but an hour later, I'd crash and need to drink three or four cups of coffee to get my energy back.

By the time I was twenty-two, my grades were crappy, I skipped classes, and I fell behind on my homework. I got intense headaches.

I saw a doctor, who asked about my diet and concluded I had both a caffeine and a sugar addiction. He said I'd need to break them. Food addictions, as it turns out, are increasingly the focus of scientific studies. Experiments with animals and humans have shown that "highly palatable foods" rich in sugar or salt trigger the same reward and pleasure centers of the brain as cocaine and heroin. That feel-good dopamine issues from the brain, people feel great, and immediately they want to eat some more.

It angers me now to think back on that time. This was before the internet, and I had no idea sugar and high-glycemic carbohydrates were so bad for you. The products

I ate—the chocolate milk, the Zingers, the Pepsis, and the M&M's—were developed by food scientists. They were well aware of the effects their products had on a person's body. These food scientists were engineering food addictions in millions of people like me.

You do things because they feel good. You eat things because they taste good. Chocolate milk and Zingers tasted delicious to me. I never thought for a second I was poisoning myself.

They say a journey of a thousand miles starts with a single step, and going to the doctor was my first step. Once I knew the culprits of my malaise, it became a process of eliminating them.

That, I learned, was easier said than done.

TAKING THE NEXT STEPS

I switched my breakfast from Zingers and chocolate milk to a bowl of cereal. I also quit smoking. Still, I suffered from midmorning and midafternoon fatigue, and I still had yo-yo weight. I cut back on caffeine and suffered withdrawal symptoms, including headaches, nausea, and fatigue.

I had trouble eliminating sugar, because there weren't

many options at the time. I switched to diet sodas, like Diet Coke and Diet Pepsi, because they were sweetened with the sugar substitute saccharin, which you'd also find in the pink packets of Sweet'n Low. This change didn't help me lose weight or feel better. I still didn't have much energy.

When dealing with food addiction—like any other addiction—you must be cautious about the people you surround yourself with. If you're a drug addict and hanging around with people still using drugs, you're more likely to use again. If you're an alcoholic hanging out with drinkers, you fall off the wagon. In my case, all my college friends still drank soda and snacked on Pringles, Fritos, Cheetos, and candy bars. It took me four years to find a different group of people and break the bad habits I'd created.

After I finished college and started working, I continued to struggle with my weight. Then, in 1994, when I was in my midthirties, I read *Dr. Atkins' Diet Revolution*, and a light went on for me.

Atkins's diet is low in carbohydrates and high in protein and fats. Atkins developed it as an answer to the obesity, type 2 diabetes, and heart disease problems he felt were caused by the typical American diet that is low in fat and high in carbohydrates. Atkins believed sugar, white flour, and other refined carbohydrates led to blood sugar imbalances, weight gain, and cardiovascular problems.

At the time I discovered Atkins, the US Department of Agriculture's dietary pyramid encouraged grains, carbs, and sugar as the basis of your diet. For someone like me, who had suffered from eating too much sugar, the Atkins diet's emphasis on low carbs and little sugar[1] enticed me more than government-recommended food pyramids.

I lost weight—when I stayed on the diet. I'd be on a keto diet for three months, and I'd lose twenty pounds. I'd feel good and then go off the diet. I'd gain the weight back until I got so fat I couldn't stand it anymore. Then I'd go back on the keto diet and lose twenty pounds. Then I'd go off it again.

This went on for years, until that fateful morning when I woke up in the Luxor in Las Vegas. That's when I understood: I couldn't just diet. I had to commit to adopting the ketogenic lifestyle.

THE DIET SODA TRAP

When I became serious about adopting the ketogenic lifestyle, I still drank diet sodas. Like everyone else, I thought no-calorie artificial sweeteners would not affect

---

1   In my mind, an Atkins diet is synonymous with a ketogenic diet. Atkins has been around for forty years, and ketogenics is a recently coined term for essentially the same thing: a diet that is low in carbohydrates, moderate in protein, and high in fat. Both follow the same principles and have the same result. Your body burns more fat for energy, and you are less likely to suffer the health problems associated with a high carbohydrate diet.

my blood sugar levels and would help me lose weight by keeping me in ketosis, burning fat for energy instead of sugars or carbs.

But as I read all I could about diet and the benefits of a ketogenic lifestyle, I kept coming across studies debunking the myth that diet sodas would not contribute to obesity. A study in the *Yale Journal of Biology and Medicine* published in 2010 noted that the percentage of the population that is obese has grown in tandem with the increased use of artificial sweeteners, such as the aspartame in Diet Coke and the sucralose in Pepsi One. Other studies noted by the National Institutes of Health suggested a link between artificially sweetened beverage consumption and weight gain in children. Another 2010 article in the journal *Neuroscience* concluded artificial sweeteners encourage sugar cravings. A 1986 study in *Lancet* found aspartame stimulates appetite and leads to weight gain.

After reading these and other studies, I decided to conduct a test on whether diet sodas affected my blood sugar levels. My experiment:

- Do a five- to six-hour fast without eating in the evening.
- Drink a Diet Pepsi or Diet Coke.
- Go to bed.
- Check my blood sugar in the morning.

The results: my blood sugar was elevated the next morning after drinking a soft drink with aspartame. Why would this be so? I had not consumed actual sugars. Why would my body behave as if I had?

Based on my experiment results, I cut out aspartame. Next, I experimented with sucralose, the sweetener used in Splenda. Food manufacturers create sucralose by treating a sugar molecule with chlorine gas. This changes the molecular structure of the sugar so your body isn't supposed to recognize it as sugar, and it passes through your system (or so they say). However, my experiment (with the same conditions as the one with aspartame) bore the same results: my blood sugar the next morning was elevated at the same rate as it was with aspartame.

I concluded that drinking soft drinks that contain aspartame or sucralose will kick you out of ketosis and will raise your blood sugar levels, although not as much as with sugared drinks. It helped me understand why so many people continued to be obese even when no-calorie, artificial sweeteners flooded the market.

ADDED SUGAR HIDES IN PACKAGED FOODS

Over time, I learned food manufacturers use sugar and artificial sweeteners in a wide variety of foods—not just sweets and desserts. I started studying the labels on the food I bought. I was stunned. Spaghetti sauces, salsas, and condiments all contain huge amounts of sugar. Three tablespoons of ketchup—enough to put on your burger and still give you something to dip your fries into—has more sugar than a Krispy Kreme donut, according to an article in the *Huffington Post*. Sweet chili sauce, the stuff you get at Thai restaurants, has 30 percent more sugar than ketchup.

Most people probably aren't aware of this. Even if you skip dessert, you may still consume more added sugar than is recommended.

Almost all processed food, I learned, contains some form of sugar. If it's in a box or a can, it probably contains sugar. Even those foods that claim to be low-calorie foods contain artificial sugars, which from my experience is just as bad. This helped explain why I could be watching calories by eating low-calorie foods and drinking diet sodas and still have trouble losing weight. I had success with ketogenic diets, but hidden sugars were throwing me out of ketosis and causing me to gain weight.

This is when I realized that to succeed I would need to do two things:

- Read labels so I could avoid food with hidden sugars.

- Commit not just to a ketogenic diet but to a ketogenic lifestyle.

I only shop in the outside aisles of the supermarket where stores keep all the fresh products high in nutrients. I avoid the inside aisles filled with the boxes, jars, and cans more likely to contain sugar. In some cases, like with ketchup and salad dressings and so forth, they contain far more sugar than you imagined.

HOW DO I KNOW IF I'M EATING ADDED SUGAR?

There's only one way to know: read the label.

The US Food and Drug Administration (FDA) requires food producers to list all ingredients in their foods. But added sugar comes in many forms, and there are at least sixty-one different names for sugar listed on food labels. No wonder sugar is so hard to find on the ingredients label.

SIXTY-ONE NAMES FOR SUGAR YOU MAY FIND ON THE INGREDIENT LABEL

Agave nectar

Barbados sugar

Barley malt

Barley malt syrup

Beet sugar

Brown sugar

Buttered syrup

Cane juice

Cane juice crystals

Cane sugar

Caramel

Carob syrup

Castor sugar

Coconut palm sugar

Coconut sugar

Confectioner's sugar

Corn sweetener

Corn syrup

Corn syrup solids

Date sugar

Dehydrated cane juice

Demerara sugar

Dextrin

Dextrose

Evaporated cane juice

Free-flowing brown sugars

Fructose

Fruit juice

Fruit juice concentrate

Glucose

Glucose solids

Golden sugar

Golden syrup

Grape sugar

HFCS (High-Fructose Corn Syrup)

Honey

Icing sugar

Invert sugar

Malt syrup

Maltodextrin

Maltol

Maltose

Mannose

Maple syrup

Molasses

Muscovado

Palm sugar

Panocha

Powdered sugar

Raw sugar

Refiner's syrup

Rice syrup

Saccharose

Sorghum Syrup

Sucrose

Sugar (granulated)

Sweet Sorghum

Syrup

Treacle

Turbinado sugar

Yellow sugar

Some names may be familiar, such as sucrose (granulated sugar) and high-fructose corn syrup (found in nearly everything these days), as well as barley malt, dextrose, maltose, and rice syrup, among others.

While nutrition labels now list total sugar content, manufacturers are not required to break down the amount of sugar that comes from natural ingredients, such as fruit or milk, and those from "added sugar." Manufacturers add sugar to processed food to keep it fresh longer, keep jellies and jams from spoiling, help the fermentation of bread and alcohol, and improve the flavor, color, or texture of certain foods and drinks.

The Food and Drug Administration has established daily reference values—numerical guidelines for daily intake—for many macronutrients like carbohydrates, fat, protein, and salt. But it hasn't issued a value for sugar. So we don't have recommendations for how much (or how little) sugar we should be consuming, and we don't have much information on how much added sugar a product contains. This trend might change in 2020. Although it was supposed to change in 2018, the FDA pushed it out further so food manufacturers could prepare. One of the biggest changes will be the reporting of "added sugars." Added sugars will be reported in grams and as "percent daily value" and will be included on the label. The FDA is standing by its conclusion that scientific data shows it is difficult to meet nutrient needs while staying within calorie limits. However, if you consume more than 10 percent of your total daily calories from added sugar, and this is consistent with the 2015–2020 Dietary Guidelines for Americans, this puts you outside the recommended level of added sugar. Not a big step, but, nonetheless, a step in the right direction.

When obesity and diabetes are such a huge problem in this country and those ailments are so linked to sugar consumption, you'd think health officials would be more proactive. Some are: the American Heart Association, for example, recommends men consume no more than nine teaspoons (38 grams) of added sugar a day and that women consume no more than six teaspoons (25 grams) a day. Children should have no more than three to six teaspoons (12 to 20 grams) a day, depending on their size and caloric needs.

How much sugar is that? Not a lot. Some twelve-ounce sodas, for example, contain eleven teaspoons (46.2 grams) of sugar.

They put health warnings on alcohol and tobacco products, but these sweet soda bombs provide no warning whatsoever. Even if you live New York City, whose Board of Health attempted to limit the size of sugary drinks sold in cups to sixteen ounces, it's up to individuals to make careful decisions about what they eat and how much sugar they consume.

One thing you should know before you go any further is you will have to cut all sugar out of your diet, particularly fructose. Fructose could possibly be the most antiketogenic sugar of all the sugars. It is not metabolized anywhere but the liver because none of your other organs have the ability to produce the enzymes required to metabolize it. Fructose refills liver glycogen rapidly, and this will quickly knock you out of ketosis. Avoid it. Instead, consider stevia or monk fruit, which is more of a nut than a fruit.

Cutting out fructose means avoiding fruits. It is better to consume ten grams of gummy bears, M&M's, or just about any other sugar than it is to consume ten grams of fruit. Fifty percent of the carbs in fruit are fructose. You should also avoid glucose, although glucose can go to muscles instead of the liver, allowing liver glycogen to remain empty.

EVEN "HEALTHY" FOODS CAN BE HIGH IN SUGAR

You don't need a thirty-two-ounce Big Gulp or a Krispy Kreme donut to get a lot of sugar. Here are a few other products that pack a lot of sugar:

- A popular yogurt contains seven teaspoons (29 grams) of sugar per serving.

- A breakfast bar that, according to its label, is made with "real fruit" and whole grains. It has fifteen grams of sugar.
- A breakfast cereal company promises a certain bran cereal with raisins has "no high-fructose corn syrup." What it doesn't advertise is that a single serving contains twenty grams of sugar.
- One particular cranberry/pomegranate juice product that boasts of having "no high-fructose corn syrup" contains thirty grams of added sugar, mostly fructose, per eight-ounce serving. That's more than the AHA-recommended limit for a woman in an entire day.

AMERICANS CONSUME AN AVERAGE OF SIXTY-SIX POUNDS OF ADDED SUGAR EACH YEAR

According to health scientists from the University of California, San Francisco (UCSF), Americans consume an average of sixty-six pounds of added sugar a year. Every day, Americans consume on average three times more sugar than the American Heart Association recommends.

The overconsumption of sugar, the scientists say, leads to type 2 diabetes—a disease that afflicts thirty million people in the US—and extra body weight that puts a strain on a person's heart.

UCSF experts agree that manufacturers hide sugars in

processed-food labels, and that consumers have a hard time making decisions without "clearer recommendations on how much added sugar is safe to consume."

HOW POPULAR SWEETENERS STACK UP

Although sugars found in food or sold as sweeteners go by dozens of names, here is a breakdown of the eleven most popular ones, along with information on whether the sugar works in a ketogenic diet, its glycemic index,[2] how many calories it packs, its source, and the truth about the sugar. This data comes from a variety of sources, including the University of California, San Francisco; the Alliance Work Partners, a nonprofit employee-assistance network based in Texas; the federal Food and Drug Administration; and the University of Sydney in Australia.

Only the first four on this list fit in the keto lifestyle.

Stevia leaf extract
Keto: Yes
Brand names: Steviva, SteviaSweet, Sweet Leaf, and others
Calories: 0
Glycemic Index: 0

---

2   The Glycemic Index Foundation defines "glycemic index" (GI) as a relative ranking of carbohydrates in foods according to how they affect blood glucose levels. Carbohydrates with a GI value of fifty-five or less are considered low because they are digested more slowly and slowly increase blood glucose and insulin levels.

Found in: Diet drinks, yogurts, individual packets

The truth: Stevia leaf extract, also called steviol glycosides, is considered by many food scientists to be the natural alternative to artificial sweeteners. It is two hundred to four hundred times sweeter than sucrose, the FDA reports. Stevia leaves and crude stevia extracts are not permitted for use as sweeteners by the FDA, but refined stevia products such as SteviaSweet and Sweet Leaf gained a "Generally Regarded as Safe" (GRAS) approval from the FDA in 2008.

Monk Fruit Extract

Keto: Yes

Brand names: MonkSweet, Lakanto

Calories: 0

Glycemic Index: 0

Found in: Diet drinks, yogurts, individual packets

The truth: Derived from luo han guo or monk fruit, an herbaceous perennial vine native to southern China and northern Thailand. The fruit extract is three hundred times sweeter than sucrose and has been used in China as a low-calorie sweetener for cooling drinks and in traditional Chinese medicine.

Neotame

Keto: Yes

Calories: 0

Glycemic Index: 0

Found in: Some drinks, dairy products, frozen desserts, puddings, and fruit juices

The truth: This artificial sweetener was approved by the FDA in 2002. It is between seven thousand and thirteen thousand times sweeter than table sugar (depending on what it is added to) and is produced by the same company (NutraSweet) that makes aspartame. Although neotame can be part of a ketogenic diet, it is not yet widely used in the production of food products. It is the only artificial sweetener considered safe by the Center for Science in the Public Interest (CSPI).

Sugar alcohols

Keto: Yes

AKA: Erythritol, sorbitol, xylitol, mannitol

Calories: 10 per teaspoon

Glycemic Index: From 1 (erythritol) to 12 (xylitol)

Found in: Sugar-free candies, gum, desserts

The truth: Sugar alcohols have 2.6 calories per gram. Sugar alcohols are not as sweet and caloric as sugar, but consuming large amounts can cause bloating and diarrhea. Sugar alcohols are often used in sugar-free foods marketed to diabetics, but they do contain some carbohydrates and an excess amount may increase blood sugar. The American Heart Association recommends consuming sugar alcohols in moderation and counting half of the grams of sugar alcohols as carbohydrates because only about half get digested.

The rest of these sweeteners do not help keep you in ketosis.

Sucrose, or table sugar

Keto: No

Glycemic Index: 65

Calories: 16 per teaspoon

Found in: fruit; added to baked goods, jams, marinades, salad dressings

The truth: Sucrose offers energy but no nutritional benefits.

Acesulfame potassium

Keto: No

Brand names: Sunett, Sweet One

Calories: 0

Glycemic Index: 0

Found in: Soft drinks, gelatins, chewing gum, frozen desserts

The truth: A nonnutritive artificial sweetener, acesulfame potassium was first approved by the FDA in 1988. It does not break down under high temperatures and is used in thousands of processed food products. Premarket testing was sparse. Hoescht, the manufacturer of the chemical, ran a few long-term animal studies that showed it might be linked to cancer (although animal studies don't always translate to humans).

Agave nectar

Keto: No

Calories: 20 per teaspoon

Glycemic Index: 15

Found in: Cereals, yogurts, tea

The truth: The nectar is a product of the agave cactus, and its taste and texture are similar to honey. It doesn't contain as many antioxidants as honey, but it contains approximately the same number of calories. Agave, however, is sweeter than sugar, so proponents suggest you can use less to get similar sweetness. Agave nectar contains more fructose than table sugar, which means it's less likely to cause a spike in blood sugar. But it will take you out of ketosis.

Aspartame

Keto: No

Brand names: Equal, NutraSweet

Calories: 0

Glycemic Index: 0

Found in: Drinks, gum, yogurt, cough drops

The truth: As one of the most studied artificial sweeteners, aspartame has been accused of causing everything from weight gain to cancer. Since FDA approval in 1981, however, studies have found no convincing evidence of this. The FDA, the World Health Organization, and the American Dietetic Association say aspartame in moderation poses no threats. CSPI gave aspartame its lowest ranking in a review of food additives. People with phenylketonuria, an inherited genetic disorder, should avoid it for fear of coma.

Honey

Keto: No

Calories: 21 per teaspoon

Glycemic Index: 50

Found in: Cereals, baked goods, teas

The truth: Honey contains trace amounts of vitamins and minerals, and it may not raise blood sugar as fast as other sweeteners. This is beneficial because it's better for the body to have a slow and steady rise in blood sugar after eating, rather than a dramatic spike. Honey contains calories and should be used as sparingly as any other full-calorie sweeteners. A folk remedy suggests a few teaspoons of honey an hour before bed can bring a restful sleep.

Saccharin

Keto: No

Brand names: Sweet'n Low

Calories: 0

Glycemic Index: 0

Found in: Drinks, canned goods, candy

The truth: Studies on rats in the seventies linked saccharin to bladder cancer. Congress mandated in 1981 that all foods containing it have a warning label. Later studies failed to link saccharin to cancer in humans, however, so Congress later repealed the warning label.

Sucralose

Keto: No

Brand name: Splenda

Calories: 0

Glycemic Index: 0

Found in: Fruit drinks, canned fruit, syrups

The truth: Sucralose was created in an experiment in which a sugar molecule was treated with chlorine gas. According to *Eurekas and Euphorias: The Oxford Book of Scientific Anecdotes*, researchers were looking for ways to use synthetic derivatives of sucrose for industrial purposes. It was never meant to be a sweetener, but then a scientist tasted the derivative and found it was powerfully sweet. Sucralose is between three hundred to one thousand times sweeter than sugar. In its pure state, it doesn't have any calories, although it's typically added to the bulking agent maltodextrin, which has four calories per teaspoon and a high glycemic index. Sucralose received FDA approval in 1998. It is heat stable and can be used in baking, and it's useful for people who are dieting or have diabetes.

BULKING AGENTS IN NONNUTRITIVE SWEETENERS

Many artificial sweeteners are far sweeter than sugar, so

very little is needed. Manufacturers often add them to maltodextrin, a simple carbohydrate made from starch, to bulk up the volume and make a mixture more pleasing to the mouth. Maltodextrin is added to aspartame, Splenda, and saccharin.

Maltodextrin negates the benefits of using the nonnutritive sweetener. A sweetener packet might have one part sweetener and ninety-nine parts maltodextrin. Maltodextrin has a glycemic index of 110—almost twice the number for table sugar.

HEALTH ISSUES FROM ARTIFICIAL SWEETENERS

Your body responds differently to artificial sweeteners than it does to natural or refined sugars.

The sugar substitutes erythritol, sorbitol, xylitol, monk fruit, and stevia come from natural sources. Stevia comes from a leaf. Monk fruit comes from (what else?) a fruit. Xylitol comes from birch trees. Erythritol comes from enzymatically treated or fermented sugars and is also found in nature in grape skins and cheese. Because of these natural origins, your body recognizes things like erythritol and says, "Oh, this is an alcohol sugar. We're not gonna metabolize it. We're just gonna let it run through the body."

However, your body has no instructions on how to handle

lab-created sweeteners like aspartame and sucralose. Let's say you just ate some sucralose. Your body doesn't recognize it, but it's sweet, so your body responds as if it had ingested sugar. However, as the body attempts to process this unknown compound, some adverse effects might occur.

According to *Scientific American* magazine, Israeli researchers found that ingesting artificial sweeteners might lead to obesity and diabetes. Those researchers concluded that artificial sweeteners alter intestinal bacteria and disrupt the natural metabolic transformation of food to energy. Artificial sweeteners do this by encouraging unnatural growth of the type of gut bacteria that are adept at converting that fuel into fat, researchers concluded.

Experts writing in the science journal *Gut Microbes*[3] agreed that noncaloric artificial sweeteners wreak havoc on your gut microbiome. They call it "metabolic derangement." They note that several studies have shown a "counterintuitive link" between zero-calorie sweeteners aspartame, sucralose, and saccharin and people getting fat and sick from cardiovascular disease and diabetes.

Another study by the National Institutes of Health and the American Association of Retired Persons (AARP) found

---

3   "Non-caloric artificial sweeteners and the microbiome: findings and challenges," *Gut Microbes,* April 1, 2015, https://www.ncbi.nlm.nih.gov/pmc/articles/PMC4615743/

that frequent consumption of diet drinks may increase depression in older adults. Other researchers suspect that aspartame, the chemical used in Equal and NutraSweet, will modulate brain neurotransmitters such as dopamine and serotonin.

Scientists admit there are conflicting results in many other studies on the effects of artificial sweeteners. Dr. Michael Greger, who runs a nonprofit science-based website called NutritionFacts.org, notes that Case Western University abandoned one study on the effect of aspartame on people with a history of depression. "The severity of the reactions to aspartame" by those who had previously suffered depression made it too risky to continue, Greger said.

Aspartame is composed of 50 percent phenylalanine. People with phenylketonuria (PKU), a rare disorder that causes amino acids to build up in the body, cannot metabolize phenylalanine. Doctors advise them to stay away from aspartame, which includes two amino acids. Jim May, the person that introduced me to Stevia, had a son with this condition.

Aspartame is not heat stable, so when it does get heated (like a six pack of diet soda in the back of your car on a hot day), there is some medical evidence that it can cause methanol toxicity, depression, anxiety, memory loss, headaches, or seizures. It could also exacerbate lupus, multiple sclerosis, or Parkinson's. If you look at a label of any product that contains aspartame, there's a warning on it.

THE CENTRAL LESSON

When it comes to sugar, consumers have a lot of options. But regardless of the types of sugars you choose to consume, the key is moderation. Some ingredients people think are good for them can be very harmful if you consume too much. If you try to maintain a ketogenic diet and stay in a fat-burning ketosis state, you must be even more careful.

Honey is a good example. Honey is a natural product, and its glycemic index is 50—less than table sugar. The body burns it more slowly than refined sugars like sucrose. But honey is still high in sugars, and it will give you a blood sugar spike and take you out of ketosis.

Another example is fructose. Fructose is a natural fruit sugar, and it has the lowest glycemic index (25) of all the nutritive sweeteners. Dietitians often recommend fructose for diabetics because it burns more slowly than refined sugar and doesn't cause blood sugar spikes. But even with all those advantages, you should limit your intake of fructose to ten grams a day—no more than three teaspoons. The liver metabolizes fructose, and when you exceed ten grams in one day, you run the risk of increasing your blood lipid levels and taking yourself quickly out of ketosis. That means more fat in your blood, which can lead to a buildup of unhealthy subcutaneous fat.

Many sweetened drinks now contain high fructose corn syrup. People buy it thinking they are getting a natural, healthy sugar. They aren't. High fructose corn syrup is a corn sugar, and calling it "high fructose" is a marketing ploy.

The trick is to read the labels on your food and learn how much sugar and what kind of sugar you consume. Some foods claim to be "honey-sweetened," which makes you think honey is the only sweetener used. But if you read the label, you can often find other sugars listed before honey, which means most of the sweetness in that product comes from refined, faster-burning sugars that can spike your blood sugar and throw you out of ketosis.

SWEETENING, COOKING, AND BAKING WITH ALTERNATIVE SWEETENERS

My recommendation is to sweeten, cook, and bake with the good nonnutritive sweeteners wherever possible: erythritol, stevia, xylitol, or monk fruit.

Since the sweetness varies, you must adjust your recipes.

Adjusting your recipe is easy when you use xylitol or erythritol. I prefer erythritol, because it's easier on your gastrointestinal system and it's 70 percent as sweet as sugar. If you add a little bit of stevia to the erythritol, you can get a solution that is on par with sugar, and you can use it like you would table sugar. You can also mix a little bit of monk fruit extract in with erythritol and get the same effect. It bumps up the sweetness of the erythritol.

If you use high-intensity sweeteners like stevia and monk fruit (up to two hundred times sweeter than sugar), you must adjust your recipes a lot more.

When you buy stevia or monk fruit, most companies will add maltodextrin, rice starch, or some sort of high-glycemic filler. Look for pure monk fruit extract or pure stevia extract. You can also buy a blend of stevia or monk fruit with erythritol.

In cooking and baking, there are reasons you can't always replace the sugar called for in a recipe (usually table sugar) with an artificial sweetener one for one:

- Some sweeteners aren't heat-stable.
- Many sweeteners are concentrated, so the volume will be off.
- Substitution might affect the flavor profile (might be too sweet or have unintended chemical flavors).

- The sweetener may affect mouth feel or texture of the final product.
- In baked goods, sugar contributes to caramelization or browning.

If you can't replace fully and need to use nutritive sweeteners in cooking or baking, then be cognizant of portion control. Offset the sugars and carbohydrates with a little more protein or a lot more fat in the meal.

At the end of the day, you must weigh whether the pleasure of eating the bowl of ice cream or chocolate cake is worth getting you out of the ketosis you worked so hard to get into (and the pain and suffering it's going to take to get you back in).

Chapter 4

GO NATURALLY
SWEET

I met Jim May in the eighties, shortly after moving to Arizona. Jim's son had phenylketonuria, also called PKU, which is an inherited disease that causes a certain type of amino acid to build up in your body. People with this condition lack an enzyme needed to break down phenylalanine, which is found in foods containing protein. When you suffer from PKU, your diet has to be strictly limited. You can't eat milk, cheese, chicken, nuts, beef, pork, or fish. Most patients must keep detailed food logs and get regular blood tests to ensure they aren't ingesting too much phenylalanine.

Sweet foods are a particular concern because PKU patients need to avoid the artificial sweetener aspartame, which is rich in phenylalanine and found in a lot of low-calorie processed foods. Aspartame is 50 percent phenylalanine, and it can put a PKU patient into a coma. Jim had gone on a trek to Paraguay to find herbs that might help his son overcome some of the challenges the boy lived with. He searched for a safe, natural sugar his son could eat. That search led him and his Guarani Indian guides to the stevia plant.

When Jim gave me that taste of the green stevia paste he brought back and started talking about the dangers posed by a hidden sugar like aspartame, the wizard was exposed.

I realized that all of these massive chemical companies, the food research companies, the frankenfood companies don't act in the best interest of the consumer but in the best interest of their shareholders. These companies weren't traipsing through the jungles of Paraguay to find things to keep people healthy. They were mixing up their new sugars in laboratories, looking for ways to increase profits.

Once I tasted those stevia leaves in that paste, the light bulb went off. *This doesn't have any calories. This doesn't have any carbohydrates. It doesn't affect blood sugar levels. This is amazing!* My next thought was, *How do we unlock those sweet constituents from those leaves and use that to create food products that are more natural and that are better for people?*

WAITING FOR THE FDA

I began exploring sweeteners and dreaming I could build a business that did good for the world as well as my own health. When I read Dr. Atkins's book, the ketogenic diet and natural sweetener worlds converged for me.

Although my day job was in the entertainment industry, my heart and my hustle were in growing Steviva, my company, into a global brand. I planned to launch a line of sweeteners and build a food ingredient company.

I wanted to introduce the natural version of aspartame to the world. I remember looking at all the products on shelves containing aspartame, with the little "sweetened with NutraSweet" logo with the little peppermint. I thought, "No. My logo is the future."

But I didn't realize the wall I'd be hitting with the FDA. In 1998 the FDA would only allow stevia to be sold as a dietary supplement, not as a sweetener. We faced a long, uphill battle to change that. Throughout that entire time, I created products for myself and developed sweetening systems for baked goods and homemade condiments that would support my ketogenic, low-carb diet. I also worked on products that were safe for diabetics and people with hypoglycemia, which is when blood sugar is abnormally low, making people feel lightheaded and shaky.

It was important to me to share what I learned. This was the late nineties, and the internet was still in its infancy. I created an email newsletter called *Mind, Body, and Spirit*, and I put small ads in newspapers broadcasting that I had discovered a new sweetener and to email my company for free samples. Before long, we had over one hundred thousand people on our email list.

We still have that same newsletter today! It goes out every Sunday to 150,000 subscribers. We also have a Wednesday edition called *Supernatural Recipes* and a Friday newsletter called *Sliced Bread* that cover trends in cooking, gadgetry, and healthy living.

Finally, in 2008, Cargill, one of the largest agribusiness companies in the world, convinced the FDA to approve stevia as a sweetener. This major development allowed me to concentrate on my goals. Steviva, my company and for years my side hustle, became my primary focus.

THE SWEET TASTE OF KETOGENIC SUCCESS

As I mentioned earlier, getting a good handle on the sugars—both artificial and natural—you put in your body is only part of the process of adopting a ketogenic lifestyle. While it's true sugars and other carbohydrates can throw you out of ketosis faster than you can say "love handles," following a ketogenic lifestyle calls for other changes in your habits.

For me, one of my most important habits is my morning Hour of Power.

I wake up at 4:30 a.m., and I'll have Bulletproof Coffee. Bulletproof Coffee was made popular by Dave Asprey, a Silicon Valley executive. Bulletproof Coffee is a concoction of specialty coffee, grass-fed butter, and special coconut oil called MCT.

I make eight to twelve ounces of coffee from espresso shots or from a French press. I add one to two teaspoons of MCT oil. MCT stands for multichain triglyceride, and it's an efficient, high-quality fat derived from coconut oil. It's rocket fuel for your brain and wakes it up. I also add one to two teaspoons of grass-fed, unsalted butter or ghee (clarified butter). I prefer ghee over butter because it's 100 percent pure butterfat, with all the lactose and casein removed. If you are lactose intolerant, you can have ghee. Ghee is useful in other ways. Its high smoke point (485 degrees) allows you to cook with it at very high temperatures.

Finally, I'll add some of my sweetener to my Bulletproof Coffee and put it in the blender for twenty seconds. It turns out like a latte. All the fat goes straight to your brain, and you have absolute clarity.

One word of caution: too much MCT oil may lead to what

Tim Ferriss calls "disaster pants." When I first started taking MCT oil, my attitude was, "Well, if some is good, then a lot is better!" This was early in my ketogenic journey, and I decided to add a little extra MCT oil to my coffee before I went for a 5 a.m. walk with my dog. About halfway through my walk, I realized I had to go now, and it was so urgent I had to duck behind a bush. It happened again the next day, but I did some research and discovered other people associating disaster pants with too much MCT. Lesson learned. MCT oil is a shortcut to adding fat to your diet and putting yourself in ketosis, but it could lead to a messy situation.

A COMPLETE WORKOUT

My Hour of Power, which takes much longer than an hour, sets the stage for my day. This is the time of day when I reflect, sweat, stretch, think, and meditate.

An Hour of Power may seem daunting when you're just starting out. It's great to push yourself, but better yet, nudge yourself at first. Everybody starts at the beginning. When I began this process, I could barely do five push-ups, but over time, I ramped up my Hour of Power until I was doing dozens of push-ups and sit-ups.

Start slowly and work your way up. Don't hurt yourself because that will keep you from going back to it. Any amount of exercise and movement can benefit your mindset and weight loss goals.

Before I go into details, let me say that the Hour of Power shifts my mindset from a fixed mindset to a growth mindset. In a fixed mindset, you see a situation as negative and unchanging. You see yourself as a victim, that things happen to you and that you have no control over them. If you're in that fixed mindset, you'll never be successful making a change in your lifestyle. You think:

- I'm always going to be fat.
- I'm always going to feel poorly about myself.
- I'm never going to have that relationship.

With a growth mindset, anything seems possible. You will make it probable. I encourage you to get one of the greatest books ever written about developing a strong mentality: *Mindset* by Carol Dweck. Having a growth-oriented mindset is what's going to make you successful in a lifestyle change.

WEIGHING IN

I weigh myself as soon as I get out of bed and write the number in my journal. I also analyze my weight:

- If my weight goes down, I look at what I did in previous

days to cause it. Did I work out longer earlier in the week? Did I stop eating after 6:00 p.m.?

- If my weight goes up, I reflect on the things that may have caused that. Late dinners? Extra snacks? Curtailed workouts?

When I record my weight in my journal, I also jot down my thoughts on how I'm feeling, how well I slept, and what challenges I'm facing in the coming day. I create my roadmap.

JOURNALING

I started journaling about twenty years ago. I have made it a daily practice and weave it into the fabric of my Hour of Power. This journal is sacred to me. I have stacks upon stacks of them in storage. It's awesome to go back in time and see where I was, who I was with, what I was doing, and what I was struggling with. It is really an amazing habit. Journaling has helped me and accelerated my personal growth exponentially. Aside from scribing my daily musings, I use it to collect data on my Hour of Power, my weight, changes in my physique, and sometimes a reflection on what I can do better. I can't recommend journaling enough. It will help you clear your head, chart a course, and face the day with exuberance. Though it may sound like a modality for mental health, it can really keep you on track with your lifestyle change.

MORNING RUN

After I've journaled, I grab my dog, and I go for a three-and-a-half-mile run. If you consider a similar regimen, don't think you must start running this far. If you haven't been running or doing any exercise, start slowly and build up over time. When I first started my Hour of Power, I walked and only went half a mile. Over time I increased my distance to one mile of walking and then two. Then I added in periods of jogging. After several months, I had a standard three-and-a-half-mile route, and I ran the entire way.

CYCLE AND PODCASTS

After my run, I cycle for at least twenty minutes on my stationary bike. While I'm pedaling, I keep a growth mindset and positive attitude by listening to audiobooks and podcasts. Some favorite podcasts are:

- Lewis Howes, *School of Greatness*
- Tom Bilyeu, *Impact Theory*
- Gary Vaynerchuk, *Gary Vaynerchuk Audio Experience*
- Tim Ferriss, *The Tim Ferriss Show*
- James Altucher, *The James Altucher Show*
- Joe Rogan, *The Joe Rogan Experience*

I listen to any podcast that's going to send me a positive message about the hustle and the grind and help me get myself even more pumped up for the day. I am quite certain I will be adding to this list, so check in on my website to see what I am listening to now.

DUMBBELL WORKOUT

Next, I do a dumbbell workout with curls, presses, and flies. I started with fifteen-pounders, but now I'm up to twenty-five-pounders. Dumbbells are cheap—you can get yourself a set on Amazon for twenty or thirty bucks.

KETTLEBELL WORKOUT

Tim Ferriss's podcast got me interested in the kettlebell workout. The kettlebell isn't just for fat burning. It's a strength-builder that some of the world's mightiest lifters swear by. Pavel Tsatsouline brought it over from Russia. In Pavel's words, "The kettlebell doesn't care about your age, weight, or background. He wants you to pick him up." So I did. Using proper form is key. Before you start swinging around the kettlebell and fixing elections like a mad Russian, research it. Don't overdo it. The kettlebell will kick your ass. But if you start out easy—I started with fifteen pounds—it will whip you into shape faster than a set of burpees.

SIT-UPS AND PUSH-UPS

I started with ten sit-ups, and now I do three sets of seventy-five sit-ups.

When I first started, I could only do ten knee push-ups. (Yes, I journaled that.) Within a couple weeks, I was up to fifteen regular push-ups. A couple weeks later, I got up to twenty. As I got stronger, I started doing my push-ups on a BOSU ball because the instability works short-twitch muscles for a better workout. Now I do three sets of fifty push-ups on the BOSU ball.

YOGA

I try to practice yoga daily because I find that:

1. It's a great way to get fit.
2. It incorporates breathing exercises that boost metabolism.

A lot of people under stress hold their breath. When you practice focused breathing along with the relaxed movements of yoga, it helps the flow of oxygen, feeds your cells, and revitalizes you.

MEDITATION

After my yoga, I meditate for a minimum of ten minutes.

If you've never meditated, phone apps can help you get started. Here are the basics: either sit or lie down and take ten minutes to breathe and to allow your thoughts to roll in and roll out. Don't judge your thoughts. Allow them to be.

Meditation is a perfect crescendo to your morning Hour of Power. You go out to face the world with a solid foundation.

People ask if the Hour of Power is best done in the morning. My answer is yes.

The Hour of Power mentally sets the tone for the day. But morning is best for a physical reason: you've been fasting all night, and you're in ketosis by morning. Working out first thing fires up your engine and burns fat. You can have coffee or whatever warm beverage you have in the morning, but no food. Eating interferes with the process.

I wrap up my day with a three-and-a-half-mile walk in the evening with my dog. Walking is a terrific way to get fresh air and relax. Bring a family member, friend, or somebody in your support group. A long walk is a great time to have conversations.

LEVELING UP

I'm an achiever, so I always try to improve by running farther or adding reps. Seeing improvement creates excitement and motivation to do more. When you look in the mirror and see muscles getting toned, you wonder what results even harder workouts might bring.

Your efforts will affect the people in your life. They will level up, too. You will empower other people to change and improve.

After I started seeing the results of fitness and a ketogenic lifestyle, I felt obligated to share these habits with my customers, friends, and the world. I feel like I've received a second chance, and I feel like I must share my experience with others. If I can impact just one other person's life, that will be a huge success for me.

One of my customers, Dan Sullivan, shared his own success with me. On January 1, 2016, Dan weighed 310 pounds, the heaviest he had ever been. Dan had dieted before, but never in a way he felt he could sustain. So he researched the ketogenic approach because he'd had success in the past with the Atkins diet.

"I also became very interested in gut health," Dan wrote to me. "I adopted a keto diet in April of 2016. At the end of 2016, my weight was 250 pounds."

I was also happy to hear Dan say that Steviva products had played a part in his success.

"My coworkers who traveled with me were accustomed to seeing my little green bottle come out of my backpack to sweeten my coffee every morning. I have plateaued since the end of last year and strayed a bit from the strict keto approach. But as I read your newsletter, I realized I had to recommit myself to track my carbs and stay strict on my twenty-five-gram limit."

It's great Dan is refocusing on his ketogenic diet. In the next chapter, I'm going to set you up with some delicious recipes that will help you do the same.

Ready? Get your aprons out!

Part III

———

LET'S EAT

Chapter 5

___

KETO MEAL PLAN

The ketogenic diet is designed to limit your intake of carbohydrates. When your body is deprived of simple carbohydrates and sugars, it increases its production of ketone bodies and burns fat for energy rather than the blood glucose that comes from carbohydrates. The result is you lose weight, reduce body fat, and stand a better chance of avoiding health issues related to obesity, diabetes, and cardiovascular disease. That fat-burning state is called ketogenesis and can result from consuming less than twenty grams of net carbohydrates a day.

"Net carbs" is a term used by food manufacturers to account for certain foods containing fiber and sugar alcohols that don't have a big impact on blood sugar levels. Net carbs are equal to a food's total carbohydrate content minus the fiber and sugar alcohols that those foods contain but that pass through the body without being digested.

For example, simple or refined sugars and starches like potatoes, white bread, sweets, and white rice are quickly absorbed by the body and have a high glycemic index, meaning they cause blood sugar levels to go up rapidly after they are consumed. Any of these carbohydrates that are not burned up by activity will be stored as body fat. For these foods, their net carbs are almost equal to their total carbs.

On the other hand, a large portion of the carbohydrates in healthier foods like fruits, whole grains, and vegetables is insoluble fiber. Only a portion of these carbohydrates are digested and absorbed, and the carbohydrates in them move through the digestive system more slowly, giving them a lower glycemic index. The remaining carbs move through the body as fiber. Consequently, food manufacturers have started subtracting those insoluble carbs from the total amount of carbohydrates in the food to produce a "net carbs" measurement—the portion of the food that produces energy and affects blood sugar.

Sugar alcohols like mannitol, sorbitol, and xylitol, which are used as artificial sweeteners and have no glycemic index, are also subtracted from the total carbohydrates to determine a food's net carbohydrates.

The following meal plan was compiled and analyzed by a doctor. It breaks down the macronutrients and nutritional information for each meal and snack, including calories, sugars, fats, proteins, carbs, and more.

The following meal plan calls for greater than 70 percent of calories to come from fat, 20 percent or less from protein, and less than 10 percent from the net carbohydrates coming from cruciferous vegetables grown above ground. The meal plan calls for zero calories from sweeteners because we'll be using natural, keto-friendly, nonnutritive sweeteners.

Sweetening component: No added calories from sweeteners.

Final macronutrient average results for entire meal plan:

- Fat: 72 percent
- Protein: 23 percent
- Net Carbs: 5 percent

Steviva Brands keto-friendly (nonnutritive) sweeteners:

- Steviva Blend
- SteviaSweet (100 percent Stevia) (1.3 oz.)
- SteviaSweet RA98
- SteviaSweet 95-60
- MonkSweet+

- XeroSweet

SEVEN-DAY MEAL PLAN

Recipes in this meal plan are designed for a varying number of people. Single-serving recipes can be multiplied to accommodate more people, and multiple-serving recipes can be divided for fewer people. You're free to mix and match as you see fit. Have the lunches for dinner or munch on the snacks when you'd like. The key is to stick to the proportions presented here. The order you eat them in is up to you!

The recipes in this plan are made from ingredients you're likely to already have around the house. There are a few special ingredients you may need to get, such as:

- Unsalted, grass-fed butter (like Kerrygold)
- Ghee (clarified butter)
- MCT oil
- Guar gum
- Coconut vinegar
- Egg white protein powder
- Unflavored gelatin packets
- StevivaBlend Fine Powder
- PreBiotica Inulin
- Steviva Blend

THE MEAL SCHEDULE

WEEKDAY	BREAKFAST	MIDDAY	LUNCH	DINNER	DESSERT
SUNDAY	(2) Baked Personal Omelet	(1 c.) Stevia-Sweetened Bulletproof Coffee	(1/2 recipe) Zesty Turkey Meatballs with Bok Choy	(1/2 recipe) Mediterranean Chicken Spinach Taco Bowl	(1/2 recipe) Chocolate Chia Pudding
MONDAY	(1/2 recipe) Keto Scramble	(1.5 c.) Pork Rinds with (1 Tbsp.) Tahini	(1/2 recipe) Teriyaki Chicken with Broccoli	(1x recipe) Stuffed Banana Peppers	(1 c.) Stevia Marshmallows
TUESDAY	(1) Keto Vanilla Smoothie	(1) Pumpkin Seeds and Coffee	(1/2 recipe) Grilled Portabella Burgers	(1/6 recipe) Hamburger Salad	(1) Low Carb Pudding
WEDNESDAY	(2) Egg Clouds and Bacon	(1 c.) Stevia-Sweetened Bulletproof Coffee	(1/4 recipe) Bacon-Fried Brussels Sprouts with Chicken	(1/4 recipe) Turkey Meatballs on Cauliflower Rice	(1 square) Almond Butter Keto Fudge
THURSDAY	(2) Baked Personal Omelet	(1x) Pumpkin Seeds and Coffee	(1/4 recipe) Stuffed Banana Peppers	(1) Mediterranean Chicken Spinach Taco Bowl	(1/2 recipe) Chocolate Chia Pudding
FRIDAY	(1/2 recipe) Keto Scramble	(1 c.) Stevia-Sweetened Bulletproof Coffee	(1/2 recipe) Grilled Portabella Burgers	(1/2 recipe) Zesty Turkey Meatballs with Bok Choy	(1 c.) Stevia Marshmallows
SATURDAY	(2) Egg Clouds and Bacon	(1.5 c.) Pork Rinds with (1 tbsp.) Tahini	(1/6 recipe) Hamburger Salad	(1/4 recipe) Turkey Meatballs on Cauliflower Rice	(1 square) Almond Butter Keto Fudge

BREAKFASTS

Baked Personal Omelet

Servings: 6

Ingredients:

- 8 eggs
- 1/2 cup milk
- 1/2 tsp. seasoning salt
- 3 oz. cooked ham, diced
- 1/2 c. shredded cheddar cheese
- 1 c. chopped spinach
- 1 c. cooked bacon pieces
- 1 tbsp. dried minced onion

Directions:

1. Preheat oven to 350°F and grease six porcelain ramekins (3.5 inch).
2. Beat together the liquid ingredients (eggs and milk) and add seasonings, ham, cheese, spinach, bacon, and minced onion. Pour into prepared ramekins.
3. Bake uncovered at 350°F for 10–20 minutes or until eggs are set up.

LIMITS	AMOUNT PER PORTION
TOTAL CALORIES	206 calories
ADDED SUGARS	1 calorie
SATURATED FAT	51 calories
NUTRIENTS	AMOUNT PER PORTION
PROTEIN	17 g
CARBOHYDRATES	1 g
DIETARY FIBER	0 g
TOTAL SUGARS	1 g
ADDED SUGARS	0 g
TOTAL FAT	14 g
SATURATED FAT	6 g
MONOUNSATURATED FAT	5 g
POLYUNSATURATED FAT	2 g
LINOLEIC ACID	2 g
α-LINOLENIC ACID	0.1 g
OMEGA-3—EPA	1 mg
OMEGA-3—DHA	35 mg
CHOLESTEROL	249 mg

Keto Scramble

Servings: 2

Ingredients:

- 8 eggs
- 1/4 c. heavy cream
- 1/2 red onion
- 1 tomato
- 4 oz. shredded cheddar cheese
- 3 tbsp. grass-fed butter
- Salt and pepper, to taste

Directions:

1. Finely chop all vegetables and cook in the butter over medium heat for 3–5 minutes until tender.
2. Whisk the eggs with the cream and pour into pan.
3. Scramble eggs with vegetables, then add cheese and salt and pepper to taste.

LIMITS	AMOUNT PER PORTION
TOTAL CALORIES	758 calories
ADDED SUGARS	0 calories
SATURATED FAT	318 calories
NUTRIENTS	**AMOUNT PER PORTION**
PROTEIN	38 g
CARBOHYDRATES	8 g
DIETARY FIBER	1 g
TOTAL SUGARS	5 g
ADDED SUGARS	0 g
TOTAL FAT	64 g
SATURATED FAT	35 g
MONOUNSATURATED FAT	19 g
POLYUNSATURATED FAT	5 g
LINOLEIC ACID	4 g
α-LINOLENIC ACID	0.5 g
OMEGA-3—EPA	0 mg
OMEGA-3—DHA	102 mg
CHOLESTEROL	801 mg

Keto Vanilla Smoothie

Servings: 1

Ingredients:

- 2 egg yolks
- 1/2 c. cream cheese
- 1/4 c. water
- 4 ice cubes
- 1 tbsp. MCT oil
- 1/2 tsp. pure vanilla extract
- 1 tbsp. powdered Steviva Blend (or 2 dashes of stevia)

Directions:

In a blender, combine all ingredients and blend until smooth.

LIMITS	AMOUNT PER PORTION
TOTAL CALORIES	629 calories
ADDED SUGARS	0 calories
SATURATED FAT	337 calories
ALCOHOL	5 calories

NUTRIENTS	AMOUNT PER PORTION
PROTEIN	12 g
CARBOHYDRATES	6 g
DIETARY FIBER	0 g
TOTAL SUGARS	4 g
ADDED SUGARS	0 g
TOTAL FAT	62 g
SATURATED FAT	37 g
MONOUNSATURATED FAT	15 g
POLYUNSATURATED FAT	3 g
LINOLEIC ACID	3 g
α-LINOLENIC ACID	0.2 g
OMEGA-3—EPA	4 mg
OMEGA-3—DHA	39 mg
CHOLESTEROL	496 mg

Egg Clouds and Bacon

Servings: 1

Ingredients:

- 4 strips bacon
- 2 eggs
- 1/2 tsp. salt
- 1/2 tsp. garlic powder
- 1/4 tsp. pepper
- 1/4 tsp. cayenne

Directions:

1. Preheat oven to 350°F.
2. Make a bed for the egg clouds by weaving a strip of bacon over another, like the lattice of a pie. Simpler option: lay the bacon strips side-by-side, making sure to overlap sides.
3. Bake bacon strips 5 minutes.
4. While bacon is cooking, separate egg whites from yolks. Whisk egg whites until the stiff peak stage (about 5 minutes).
5. Gently fold salt and garlic powder into egg whites. Don't stir too much or you'll lose the cloud!
6. Spoon the seasoned egg whites onto the warm bacon weave to create a little cloud.

7. With a spoon, create a dip in the cloud and gently place the whole egg yolk in it.
8. Season the tops of the clouds with cayenne or paprika and pepper.
9. Place in the oven for about 10 minutes or until bacon is sizzling and the clouds have become golden.

LIMITS	AMOUNT PER PORTION
TOTAL CALORIES	299 calories
ADDED SUGARS	0 calories
SATURATED FAT	64 calories
NUTRIENTS	**AMOUNT PER PORTION**
PROTEIN	23 g
CARBOHYDRATES	1 g
DIETARY FIBER	0 g
TOTAL SUGARS	0 g
ADDED SUGARS	0 g
TOTAL FAT	22 g
SATURATED FAT	7 g
MONOUNSATURATED FAT	9 g
POLYUNSATURATED FAT	3 g
LINOLEIC ACID	3 g
α-LINOLENIC ACID	0.1 g
OMEGA-3—EPA	0 mg
OMEGA-3—DHA	51 mg
CHOLESTEROL	363 mg

MIDDAY SNACK

Stevia-Sweetened Bulletproof Coffee

Servings: 1

Ingredients:

- 2 tbsp. unsalted grass-fed butter
- 2 tbsp. coconut oil or MCT oil
- 1 c. freshly brewed organic coffee
- 1 dash of SteviaSweet (or to taste preference of stevia powder)
- 2 tbsp. heavy cream

Directions:

1. Brew coffee (espresso, drip, French press, etc.)
2. While coffee is brewing, preheat blender by pouring hot water into it. You can also use an immersion blender (stick blender). Preheat whatever container you're going to use.
3. When coffee is done brewing, empty the hot water from the now-preheated blender/container. Add coffee, butter, and coconut oil. Add SteviaSweet! Add cream if desired.
4. Blend until there is a thick layer of foam on top like a latte.

LIMITS	AMOUNT PER PORTION
TOTAL CALORIES	543 calories
ADDED SUGARS	0 calories
SATURATED FAT	405 calories
NUTRIENTS	**AMOUNT PER PORTION**
PROTEIN	1 g
CARBOHYDRATES	4 g
DIETARY FIBER	0 g
TOTAL SUGARS	1 g
ADDED SUGARS	0 g
TOTAL FAT	60 g
SATURATED FAT	45 g
MONOUNSATURATED FAT	11 g
POLYUNSATURATED FAT	2 g
LINOLEIC ACID	2 g
α-LINOLENIC ACID	0.2 g
OMEGA-3—EPA	0 mg
OMEGA-3—DHA	0 mg
CHOLESTEROL	102 mg

Pork Rinds with Tahini

Servings: 1

Ingredients:

- 1 tbsp. tahini
- 1 1/2 c. pork rinds (UTZ Pork Rinds are my favorite, and they come in huge one-pound containers! If you're not on the East Coast, you can get them online.)

NUTRIENTS	AMOUNT PER PORTION
PROTEIN	30 g
CARBOHYDRATES	3 g
DIETARY FIBER	1 g
TOTAL SUGARS	0 g
ADDED SUGARS	0 g
TOTAL FAT	16 g
SATURATED FAT	6 g
MONOUNSATURATED FAT	8 g
POLYUNSATURATED FAT	2 g
LINOLEIC ACID	2 g
α-LINOLENIC ACID	0.1 g
OMEGA-3—EPA	0 mg
OMEGA-3—DHA	0 mg
CHOLESTEROL	46 mg

Pumpkin Seeds and Coffee

Servings: 1

Ingredients:

- 1/4 c. pumpkin seeds
- 1 c. black coffee

Directions:

Enjoy a snack that is high in protein, caffeine, and fat!

LIMITS	AMOUNT PER PORTION
TOTAL CALORIES	195 calories
ADDED SUGARS	0 calories
SATURATED FAT	27 calories
NUTRIENTS	**AMOUNT PER PORTION**
PROTEIN	11 g
CARBOHYDRATES	4 g
DIETARY FIBER	2 g
TOTAL SUGARS	0 g
ADDED SUGARS	0 g
TOTAL FAT	17 g
SATURATED FAT	3 g
MONOUNSATURATED FAT	6 g
POLYUNSATURATED FAT	7 g
LINOLEIC ACID	7 g
α-LINOLENIC ACID	0.0 g
OMEGA-3—EPA	0 mg
OMEGA-3—DHA	0 mg
CHOLESTEROL	0 mg

Zesty Turkey Meatballs with Bok Choy

Servings: 2

Ingredients:

For the meatballs:

- 1 lb. ground turkey
- 2 tbsp. Italian seasoning
- 1 egg
- 2 tsp. salt
- 1 tsp. black pepper

For the zesty salad:

- 1 large bok choy cabbage, roughly chopped
- 1 c. pitted olives
- 4 cloves garlic
- 2 tbsp. olive oil

Directions:

1. Preheat oven to 350°F.
2. Mix all the meatball ingredients together to form about 12 meatballs. Place on baking sheet.
3. Bake the turkey meatballs for 30 minutes (or until internal temperature reaches 160°F).

4. Rinse and chop the bok choy, then place on a plate.
5. For the zesty dressing, combine olives, garlic, and olive oil in a food processor or blender and blend until roughly chopped/mixed together. Pour over bok choy.
6. Place meatballs on top of the bok choy.

LIMITS	AMOUNT PER PORTION
TOTAL CALORIES	425 calories
ADDED SUGARS	0 calories
SATURATED FAT	35 calories
NUTRIENTS	AMOUNT PER PORTION
PROTEIN	55 g
CARBOHYDRATES	7 g
DIETARY FIBER	2 g
TOTAL SUGARS	1 g
ADDED SUGARS	0 g
TOTAL FAT	20 g
SATURATED FAT	4 g
MONOUNSATURATED FAT	12 g
POLYUNSATURATED FAT	3 g
LINOLEIC ACID	3 g
α-LINOLENIC ACID	0.3 g
OMEGA-3—EPA	5 mg
OMEGA-3—DHA	24 mg
CHOLESTEROL	194 mg

Sugar-free Sweet and Savory Chicken

Servings: 3

Ingredients:

- 3/4 c. water
- 1/2 c. low sodium soy sauce
- 1/4 c. olive oil
- 3/4 c. Steviva Blend
- 1/4 tsp. garlic powder
- 1/8 tsp. ground ginger
- 1/8 tbsp. guar gum
- 1 lb. chicken, cubed
- 1 lb. broccoli florets

Directions:

1. In a saucepan over medium-high heat, whisk together water, soy sauce, Steviva Blend, garlic powder, ginger, and guar gum.
2. Bring to a boil, stirring constantly, until mixture thickens slightly.
3. Cook the chicken in a little olive oil until fully cooked. Pour sauce over top and mix.
4. Steam broccoli thoroughly. Place on plate. Cover broccoli with chicken.

LIMITS	AMOUNT PER PORTION
TOTAL CALORIES	444 calories
ADDED SUGARS	0 calories
SATURATED FAT	33 calories
NUTRIENTS	**AMOUNT PER PORTION**
PROTEIN	51 g
CARBOHYDRATES	7 g
DIETARY FIBER	2 g
TOTAL SUGARS	1 g
ADDED SUGARS	0 g
TOTAL FAT	24 g
SATURATED FAT	4 g
MONOUNSATURATED FAT	15 g
POLYUNSATURATED FAT	3 g
LINOLEIC ACID	2 g
α-LINOLENIC ACID	0.2 g
OMEGA-3—EPA	6 mg
OMEGA-3—DHA	9 mg
CHOLESTEROL	145 mg

Grilled Portabella Burgers

Servings: 2

Ingredients:

- 4 portabella mushroom caps with stems removed
- 1 tbsp. balsamic vinegar
- 2 tbsp. olive oil
- 2 thin slices smoked Gouda
- 2 thick slices tomato
- Sea salt and pepper
- 1 handful basil leaves

Directions:

1. Preheat grill to medium.
2. Wash mushroom caps and dry.
3. In a shallow bowl, combine the balsamic vinegar and olive oil. Place mushrooms gill side down in the mixture.
4. When the grill is hot, grill the mushrooms on the gill side first for about 5 minutes or until they start to sweat. Flip and grill 2-3 minutes more. Add Gouda to the grill and grill 2 minutes on each side over relatively high heat until grill marks form on the cheese and it becomes soft and pliable. Sprinkle salt and pepper on the tomato to taste.
5. Assemble your portabella burgers with the mushroom

as the bun, the gouda cheese as the burger, then the lightly salted tomato and fresh basil leaves. Serve hot.

LIMITS	AMOUNT PER PORTION
TOTAL CALORIES	263 calories
ADDED SUGARS	0 calories
SATURATED FAT	63 calories
NUTRIENTS	AMOUNT PER PORTION
PROTEIN	11 g
CARBOHYDRATES	8 g
DIETARY FIBER	3 g
TOTAL SUGARS	5 g
ADDED SUGARS	0 g
TOTAL FAT	22 g
SATURATED FAT	7 g
MONOUNSATURATED FAT	12 g
POLYUNSATURATED FAT	2 g
LINOLEIC ACID	2 g
α-LINOLENIC ACID	0.2 g
OMEGA-3—EPA	0 mg
OMEGA-3—DHA	0 mg
CHOLESTEROL	27 mg

Bacon-Fried Brussels Sprouts with Chicken

Servings: 4

Ingredients:

- 1 lb. bacon, chopped
- 4 whole chicken legs, skin on
- 1 lb. Brussels sprouts, cut in half
- 2 tbsp. olive oil
- 1/2 teaspoon dried, granulated garlic or finely chopped fresh garlic
- Generous amount of black pepper and salt
- 2 tbsp. coconut vinegar
- 1/4 c. vegetable stock

Directions:

1. Preheat oven to 425°F.
2. Cook bacon in medium-hot skillet until crispy, about 8–12 minutes. Reserve bacon grease.
3. Place halved Brussels sprouts in a large bowl and drizzle them with oil and bacon grease. Season with salt and pepper or desired seasoning.
4. Generously season entire surface of chicken legs with salt and granulated garlic. Let stand for 5 minutes.
5. Fry chicken in olive oil and a little bacon grease on medium to medium-high heat until thoroughly cooked (165°F), about 6–8 minutes per side.

6. Once chicken is cooked, place it into a baking dish with Brussels sprouts, bacon, and remaining ingredients. Bake for 30 minutes.

LIMITS	AMOUNT PER PORTION
TOTAL CALORIES	538 calories
ADDED SUGARS	0 calories
SATURATED FAT	84 calories
NUTRIENTS	AMOUNT PER PORTION
PROTEIN	49 g
CARBOHYDRATES	5 g
DIETARY FIBER	2 g
TOTAL SUGARS	1 g
ADDED SUGARS	0 g
TOTAL FAT	35 g
SATURATED FAT	9 g
MONOUNSATURATED FAT	17 g
POLYUNSATURATED FAT	5 g
LINOLEIC ACID	3 g
α-LINOLENIC ACID	0.3 g
OMEGA-3—EPA	10 mg
OMEGA-3—DHA	17 mg
CHOLESTEROL	222 mg

Stuffed Banana Peppers

Servings: 4

Ingredients:

- 8 banana peppers, ends chopped off and hollowed
- 3 tablespoons olive oil
- 1 lb. Italian sausage
- 3 tbsp. grass-fed butter or ghee
- 1/2 tsp. Herbs de Provence
- 3 tbsp. yellow onions, chopped
- 1/2 c. mozzarella cheese
- 1 c. marinara sauce

Directions:

1. Preheat oven to 350°F.
2. Rub the banana peppers in olive oil, place on baking sheet, and bake for 20 minutes.
3. While peppers bake, cook sausage in skillet over medium heat until fully cooked and then add ghee or grass-fed butter, Herbs de Provence, and onions. Turn heat to low and cook for 5 minutes.
4. Remove banana peppers from oven and turn up broiler to 500°F.
5. Fill banana peppers with sausage mixture.
6. Top with mozzarella cheese.
7. Place stuffed peppers on an oven-safe plate with a

thin layer of marinara and cook for 5–10 minutes until mozzarella is hot and bubbling.

LIMITS	AMOUNT PER PORTION
TOTAL CALORIES	404 calories
ADDED SUGARS	231 calories
SATURATED FAT	138 calories
NUTRIENTS	**AMOUNT PER PORTION**
PROTEIN	19 g
CARBOHYDRATES	9 g
DIETARY FIBER	3 g
TOTAL SUGARS	3 g
ADDED SUGARS	58 g
TOTAL FAT	33 g
SATURATED FAT	15 g
MONOUNSATURATED FAT	13 g
POLYUNSATURATED FAT	3 g
LINOLEIC ACID	3 g
α-LINOLENIC ACID	0.4 g
OMEGA-3—EPA	0 mg
OMEGA-3—DHA	0 mg
CHOLESTEROL	78 mg

Hamburger Salad

Servings: 6

Ingredients:

For Salad:

- 1 lb. ground beef
- 1 tsp. sea salt
- 1/4 tsp. black pepper
- 8 oz. romaine or iceberg lettuce
- 1 c. tomatoes, chopped
- 3/4 c. shredded cheddar cheese
- 1/2 c. pickles, diced

For Dressing:

- 2 c. mayonnaise
- 4 tbsp. chili sauce (zero-carb kind)
- 4 tbsp. green bell peppers, chopped
- 4 tbsp. onion, chopped
- 2 tbsp. lemon juice
- 2 tsp. Steviva Blend
- 1 tbsp. Worcestershire sauce
- 2 hard-cooked eggs, chopped

Directions:

1. Cook ground beef in a skillet over high heat, breaking up pieces with a spatula. Season with sea salt and black pepper. Cook for 7-10 minutes, until beef is browned and moisture has evaporated.
2. Combine the remaining salad ingredients in a large bowl. Add the cooked ground beef.
3. Combine all dressing ingredients except eggs in a small blender or food processor and blend until in 1/8-inch cubes.
4. Add eggs and chill for 2 hours.

LIMITS	AMOUNT PER PORTION
TOTAL CALORIES	707 calories
ADDED SUGARS	1 calories
SATURATED FAT	135 calories
NUTRIENTS	**AMOUNT PER PORTION**
PROTEIN	18 g
CARBOHYDRATES	4 g
DIETARY FIBER	1 g
TOTAL SUGARS	2 g
ADDED SUGARS	0 g
TOTAL FAT	69 g
SATURATED FAT	15 g
MONOUNSATURATED FAT	18 g
POLYUNSATURATED FAT	33 g
LINOLEIC ACID	29 g
α-LINOLENIC ACID	4.1 g
OMEGA-3—EPA	1 mg
OMEGA-3—DHA	14 mg
CHOLESTEROL	145 mg

Mediterranean Chicken Spinach Taco Bowls

Servings: 2

Ingredients:

- 1 lb. boneless, skinless chicken breasts
- 2 tsp. Mediterranean spice blend
- 3 tbsp. balsamic vinegar
- 3 tbsp. olive oil
- 4 c. spinach, chopped
- 1 tbsp. red onion, thinly sliced
- 1/4 c. whole-fat Greek yogurt
- 1 1/2 oz. crumbled feta cheese

Directions:

1. Preheat oven broiler on high.
2. Cut chicken breasts into strips. Season chicken with 1 tsp. Mediterranean blend and broil until done (about 4–6 minutes per side).
3. Dress chicken strips with balsamic vinegar and remaining Mediterranean blend.
4. Place chopped spinach and red onions in a medium bowl, drizzle with vinegar, and toss to combine. Divide mixture evenly between two dishes.
5. Add cooked chicken to spinach bowl and garnish with remaining ingredients.

LIMITS	AMOUNT PER PORTION
TOTAL CALORIES	544 calories
ADDED SUGARS	0 calories
SATURATED FAT	60 calories
NUTRIENTS	AMOUNT PER PORTION
PROTEIN	58 g
CARBOHYDRATES	9 g
DIETARY FIBER	1 g
TOTAL SUGARS	6 g
ADDED SUGARS	0 g
TOTAL FAT	29 g
SATURATED FAT	7 g
MONOUNSATURATED FAT	18 g
POLYUNSATURATED FAT	4 g
LINOLEIC ACID	3 g
α-LINOLENIC ACID	0.3 g
OMEGA-3—EPA	17 mg
OMEGA-3—DHA	33 mg
CHOLESTEROL	154 mg

Turkey Meatballs on Cauliflower Rice

Servings: 4

Ingredients:

For cauliflower rice:

- 2 c. cauliflower florets
- salt, pepper

For meatballs:

- 1 lb. lean ground turkey
- 1 large egg
- 1 tsp. salt
- 2 tsp. garlic powder
- 2 tsp. pepper
- 2 tsp. paprika
- 4 cloves garlic, minced

For additional toppings:

- 2 tbsp. coconut oil
- 1/2 yellow onion, chopped
- 1 bunch fresh mint leaves, roughly chopped
- 1 tbsp. lemon zest
- 4 oz. goat cheese

Directions:

1. Pulse cauliflower in a food processor until it is coarsely chopped (and is approximately the size of rice). Cook cauliflower rice on medium heat in an oiled pan, covered, for 8 minutes. Season with salt and pepper to taste.
2. In a large bowl, combine the turkey, egg, spices, and garlic. Mix well with your hands to form 12 to 15 meatballs. Set aside.
3. In a skillet over medium heat, add the oil and onion. Cook, stirring occasionally for 5–8 minutes, or until onions are translucent.
4. Add meatballs to the pan. Cook on all sides until entire meatball is firm, inside to outside (cut one in half to check, but only after the 8-minute mark).
5. Divide the cauliflower rice between four serving dishes.
6. Add meatballs to each portion of the cauliflower rice and top with any of the additional toppings.

LIMITS	AMOUNT PER PORTION
TOTAL CALORIES	411 calories
ADDED SUGARS	0 calories
SATURATED FAT	139 calories
NUTRIENTS	AMOUNT PER PORTION
PROTEIN	29 g
CARBOHYDRATES	8 g
DIETARY FIBER	2 g
TOTAL SUGARS	4 g
ADDED SUGARS	0 g
TOTAL FAT	30 g
SATURATED FAT	15 g
MONOUNSATURATED FAT	7 g
POLYUNSATURATED FAT	4 g
LINOLEIC ACID	4 g
α-LINOLENIC ACID	0.2 g
OMEGA-3—EPA	15 mg
OMEGA-3—DHA	14 mg
CHOLESTEROL	144 mg

DESSERT

Chocolate Chia Pudding

Servings: 4

Ingredients:

- 1/2 c. chia seeds
- 1/2 c. heavy cream
- 1 c. water
- 2 tbsp. cocoa powder, unsweetened
- 2 tbsp. Steviva Blend Fine Powder
- 1/4 tsp. cinnamon

Directions:

1. Combine all ingredients in a medium bowl.
2. Divide mixture between four serving dishes. Let stand until the mixture thickens (about 1 hour).

LIMITS	AMOUNT PER PORTION
TOTAL CALORIES	247 calories
ADDED SUGARS	0 calories
SATURATED FAT	72 calories
NUTRIENTS	**AMOUNT PER PORTION**
PROTEIN	6 g
CARBOHYDRATES	14 g
DIETARY FIBER	11 g
TOTAL SUGARS	1 g
ADDED SUGARS	0 g
TOTAL FAT	20 g
SATURATED FAT	8 g
MONOUNSATURATED FAT	4 g
POLYUNSATURATED FAT	7 g
LINOLEIC ACID	2 g
α-LINOLENIC ACID	5.2 g
OMEGA-3—EPA	0 mg
OMEGA-3—DHA	0 mg
CHOLESTEROL	41 mg

Stevia Marshmallows

Servings: 30 Marshmallows

Ingredients:

- 2 tbsp. gelatin (about 3 packets unflavored gelatin)
- 1/2 c. cold water
- 1/2 c. Steviva Blend Fine Powder
- 1 c. hot water
- 2 tsp. vanilla extract
- 1 dash ground cinnamon
- 1 tbsp. PreBiotica Inulin

Directions:

1. Grease a 13×9-inch pan.
2. In a large bowl, mix gelatin with cold water and allow it to sit for at least 5 minutes.
3. Combine Steviva Blend Fine Powder and hot water in a saucepan and stir.
4. Heat mixture over high heat until it reaches 250°F (use candy thermometer).
5. Carefully and slowly add the hot mixture in a stream into the rehydrated gelatin. Stir in the vanilla extract, cinnamon, and inulin.
6. Whip mixture on high speed with an electric mixer (stand mixer works best) until stiff peaks form (like meringue).

7. Pour mixture into prepared pan and smooth it as much as possible.
8. Allow mixture to set up at least 6 hours (or overnight).
9. Once set, cut into 1-inch squares, and sprinkle any leftover Steviva Blend Fine Powder on top. Store in an airtight container.

LIMITS	AMOUNT PER PORTION
TOTAL CALORIES	2 calories
ADDED SUGARS	0 calories
SATURATED FAT	0 calories
ALCOHOL	1 calorie
NUTRIENTS	AMOUNT PER PORTION
PROTEIN	0 g
CARBOHYDRATES	1 g
DIETARY FIBER	0 g
TOTAL SUGARS	0 g
ADDED SUGARS	0 g
TOTAL FAT	0 g
SATURATED FAT	0 g
MONOUNSATURATED FAT	0 g
POLYUNSATURATED FAT	0 g
LINOLEIC ACID	0 g
α-LINOLENIC ACID	0.0 g
OMEGA-3—EPA	0 mg
OMEGA-3—DHA	0 mg
CHOLESTEROL	0 mg

Low-Carb Pudding

Servings: 1

Ingredients:

- 1 ripe avocado
- 1/4 tsp. Stevia powder
- 1 tbsp. MCT oil
- 1 tsp. of your favorite extract (I used vanilla)

Directions:

Combine all ingredients in a bowl and mix thoroughly. Add more stevia if 1/4 tsp. does not provide enough sweetness.

LIMITS	AMOUNT PER PORTION
TOTAL CALORIES	335 calories
ADDED SUGARS	0 calories
SATURATED FAT	132 calories
NUTRIENTS	AMOUNT PER PORTION
PROTEIN	3 g
CARBOHYDRATES	15 g
DIETARY FIBER	9 g
TOTAL SUGARS	1 g
ADDED SUGARS	0 g
TOTAL FAT	34 g
SATURATED FAT	15 g
MONOUNSATURATED FAT	14 g
POLYUNSATURATED FAT	3 g
LINOLEIC ACID	3 g
α-LINOLENIC ACID	0.2 g
OMEGA-3—EPA	0 mg
OMEGA-3—DHA	0 mg
CHOLESTEROL	0 mg

Almond Butter Keto Fudge

Servings: 4

Ingredients:

- 1/2 c. almond butter
- 1/2 c. grass-fed butter
- 1 tbsp. coconut oil
- 1/2 c. Steviva Blend (sweetener to equal 1 c. sugar)
- 1/2 c. egg white protein powder
- 2 tbsp. vanilla extract

Directions:

1. In a small saucepan on low heat, melt coconut oil, butter, and almond butter.
2. Add Steviva Blend and allow to dissolve.
3. Gradually add egg white protein powder (do not dump in all in at once or it will clump).
4. Stir in remaining ingredients and pour into a greased, 9×9-inch pan.
5. Chill until set in the refrigerator, or freeze for about an hour.
6. When set, cut into pieces and store in refrigerator.

LIMITS	AMOUNT PER PORTION
TOTAL CALORIES	379 calories
ADDED SUGARS	0 calories
SATURATED FAT	163 calories
ALCOHOL	16 calories
NUTRIENTS	AMOUNT PER PORTION
PROTEIN	9 g
CARBOHYDRATES	5 g
DIETARY FIBER	2 g
TOTAL SUGARS	2 g
ADDED SUGARS	0 g
TOTAL FAT	35 g
SATURATED FAT	18 g
MONOUNSATURATED FAT	12 g
POLYUNSATURATED FAT	3 g
LINOLEIC ACID	3 g
α-LINOLENIC ACID	0.1 g
OMEGA-3—EPA	0 mg
OMEGA-3—DHA	0 mg
CHOLESTEROL	61 mg

Chapter 6

———

GOOD CHEATS

Every lifestyle needs a little cheating. No, I'm not talking about relationships—you should know better than that. I am talking about some periodic indulgences to keep things exciting in your diet.

One habit that I am still trying to break is snacking in front of the tube or while I am working on a project. Snacks keep my fingers busy as well as my mouth. However, snacking on the keto diet can be difficult because it's easy to go over your daily carbohydrate limit.

Sunflower seeds and pumpkin seeds in the shell are my go-to fidget foods because it takes so much work to get those little buggers out that you end up burning calories to eat them. Try seeds in the shell instead of popcorn.

I am always on the hunt for new keto-friendly products,

and the best way I have found to sample them is through subscription services such as Keto Krate and Keto Box. Each month I get a big box of keto-friendly foods. Mostly the stuff is good, some of it is excellent, and a few selections are not so great, but you can see for yourself.

As I am putting to ink the final chapter of this book, we are just finishing a line of consumer products under the Guy Gone Keto brand. If you are reading this book, you are entitled to a free product. Find me on any of the social sites, email me, or pick up the phone like we did back in the eighties, and I'll get you some. We are starting off with the following keto-friendly products: Guy Gone Keto Barbeque Sauce, Guy Gone Keto Ketchup, Guy Gone Keto Steak Sauce, and Guy Gone Keto MCT Oil. Be on the lookout for at least a dozen more products in the months to come. It will be worth your while.

But since you are likely impatient like me, here are some of my favorite clean cheat foods. These delicious snacks won't throw you out of ketosis.

Quest Nutrition Quest Bars—These are hands down the best bars on the market. Perfectly keto-friendly with fats, protein, and fiber, these delicious bars are my mainstays.

Legendary Foods Nuts and Nut Butters—My friends at Legendary know their nuts. I know that sounds weird, but they do. Their nut butters contain no added sugars and are insanely delicious.

Keto Kookie—My friends at Keto Kookie kick ass. I can scarf these amazing treats, and my blood ketone levels are never affected.

Epic Provisions—A carnivorous delight. The folks at Epic make responsibly grown and harvested meat snacks that are fantastic and keto-friendly.

UTZ—UTZ is known for their potato chips, which are not keto, but their pork rinds are, and they are damn good. Crush them up and use them the way you once used breadcrumbs.

Zevia—This is my go-to soda. Sweetened with stevia, it keeps me hydrated, entertained, and in ketosis. If you are a boozer, you can spice it up a little for a low-carb cocktail (but go easy).

Guy's Award-Winning Sugar-Free BBQ Sauce—This showed up in my recent Keto Krate. Now I am using it regularly. Good stuff.

Moon Cheese and **Just the Cheese**—These are both great crispy cheesy snacks. They are tasty and keto-friendly. If you like cheese and potato chips, this will delight you.

Keto Bark—This showed up in my Keto Box a few weeks ago. It was damn good chocolate littered with pieces of almonds. Really tasty and keto-friendly.

Smart Cake—This has emerged as one of my favorite keto snacks. They are only thirty-eight calories and have no added sugars. If angel food cake and a cupcake had a keto-friendly baby, it would be a Smart Cake.

Front Porch Pecans—I ran into these while on the road when I was hangrily looking for a keto snack. These delicious pecans tamed the angry demon and kept me keto.

Elvio's Chimichurri—This was another Keto Box inclusion. This is perfect for steak, chicken, and even salmon. Delicious garlicky goodness.

Bariani Olive Oil—This was something I found while in Walnut, California. This is the real deal—not the stuff that's labeled "olive oil" but actually contains only 20 percent olive oil.

Sprouted pili nuts—My sister Gina turned me on to these. These are so rich and buttery you won't believe they are nuts.

Jerky—One of the most popular snacks on the keto diet. It's an excellent source of protein, and it's also low in carbohydrates. Don't overdo it, though. Too much protein will throw you out of ketosis. Remember: you need to balance protein and fat. My favorite brands include: **People's Choice Old Fashioned Hot & Spicy, Brooklyn Biltong Grass Fed Dried Beef,** and **Chomps Snack Sticks.**

Some of my favorite fatty fish snacks include: **Wild Planet Wild Sardines in Extra Virgin Olive Oil, Crown Prince Naturally Smoked Oysters in Pure Olive Oil,** and **Itsumo Wild Ahi Tuna in Extra Virgin Coconut Oil.**

There are a ton of new products that are making their way to the market labeled up as keto or low carb. Before eating this stuff, read the label and (more importantly) the nutritional statement. Look out for sugars, carbs, and artificial sweeteners. If you can't understand what it is, neither will your body, and it will generally act as if it is a sugar and throw your ass out of keto.

Avoid products with these ingredients on their labels:

- Soy
- Peanuts (which are not really nuts)
- Grains, including wheat, corn, rye, and barley
- Seed oils, such as canola, sunflower, and vegetable oils
- Artificial sweeteners other than stevia and monk fruit
- Added sugar and artificial chemicals, such as preservatives or flavorings

WHAT ABOUT BOOZE?

Booze of any kind will throw you out of ketosis. Ethanol, which is the version of alcohol found in wine, beer, and liquor, is metabolized in the liver. As we discussed before, your liver is responsible for producing ketones. If your liver is tied up metabolizing ethanol, it is unlikely it can produce enough ketone bodies to keep you in ketosis. Avoid alcohol. However, since drinking is an American mainstay and most people don't want to cut booze out of their lives completely, here are some guidelines to make sure you can crawl back to keto when the drink is done.

1. Skip the beer. It is the highway to high carbs and the alcohol will kick your ass way out of keto.
2. I love wine. I will have a glass or two on occasion. However, more than two will overload you with sugars and alcohol, leading to a downhill slide out of ketosis.
3. Mixed drinks are mostly mixer and will throw you out of keto in a Manhattan minute. You should never drink mixed drinks. If you just absolutely need one, try Zevia and clear booze, which has less sugar than other types.
4. Hard liquor has a lot of alcohol, so it will take you out of keto quickly. Try to dilute these with water or something without sugar.

All work and no play make Jack a dull boy. Cheat if you will, but as my friends at Quest Nutrition say, "Cheat clean."

If you bounce out of ketosis, you can crawl back. Keto always forgives (unlike significant others). It will always be waiting for you to come back after you have been bad. But, like cheating in any situation, there are always consequences. If you overdo it, you may pay with a few days of suffering. If you find yourself in this predicament, try doubling up on your fat and add some exogenous ketone salts, like beta-hydroxybutyrate. That will give you a nice spike of energy and help you get back in business.

Remember: going keto is not supposed to be torture. It is supposed to be empowering. If you find it disempowering, then you are doing something wrong. Get support. You can join Facebook groups and Meetups, join the Guy Gone Keto Brigade, or shoot me an email. I am here to help.

THE DREADED PLATEAU

I need to level with you: adopting a ketogenic lifestyle is not without its challenges. I speak from experience.

As I write this, it's just a few weeks after Christmas, and I've been stranded for eight weeks on a plateau. I'm not sure why, but I think I ate and drank too much during the holidays. I had wine, beer, and even some mixed drinks, which are about the best way I can think of to throw myself out of ketosis.

This happens. It may happen to you. None of us are perfect. When you slip like I have, you just have to pick yourself up, dust yourself off, and get back on the right road.

For me, that's meant several weeks of fasting, hydrating, working out, and refocusing. I raced to the aid of my microbiome, that little village of bacteria that resides in my gut. I am pretty sure some gangsters moved in demanding sugar and scaring off the villagers that support a healthy lifestyle, so I hit back with probiotics and fiber.

Now I'm starting to turn the corner. I see a light at the end of the dark tunnel. But the last several weeks have been a pain in the ass and discouraging as hell.

I know that I'm not alone, and you should know that, too. Plateaus are to be expected, and the secret to surviving them is to maintain your resolve and get back to the good practices that served you so well in the past as you adopted a ketogenic lifestyle.

The ketogenic lifestyle can be an effective weight-loss, energy, and clarity tool, but it does not guarantee that you will move from slovenly to slim without a few challenges along the way. A ketogenic lifestyle helps your body regulate its fat cells more efficiently, but your body may choose a homeostatic weight that is fatter than you like, and you may find yourself stuck for a bit.

Here are a few possible reasons for a plateau:

Portion control: Eating too many calories. Even though our metabolism is healthy, if we are overeating, the body won't dip as deeply into its fat stores for energy. If you eat too much protein and you have glucose tolerance problems, your body can convert protein to glucose.

Keto adaptation: This is when your body gradually uses ketones more efficiently. You may not be able to make your Ketostix—plastic strips with a small reagent area that changes color when it's dipped in urine to indicate the amount of ketones in your urine—turn purple at all. This is not a bad thing, and it does not mean you cannot lose weight or that the health advantages of a ketogenic lifestyle are gone. It may mean that you must watch portions and calories more closely.

Leptin signaling: This is when hormonally active fat cells send out a hormone whose job is to say, "I'm so hungry I could eat a horse." As you lose nonvisceral fat, there will be fewer fat cells around sending this signal to your metabolism. Not only is leptin part of the hunger system, it's also part of the reward system. When your leptin levels are low, food is even more rewarding. When your leptin levels are high, that's supposed to extinguish the reward system so that you don't need to eat so much. Food doesn't look nearly as good.

Carb creeping, cheating, and other user errors: This is when we get comfortable with our diets and experiment with expanding our palate. We lose some of the rigor that we applied when starting. The net effect is that we are eating more carbohydrates than we expect. Count those carbs, damn it.

Being too focused on weight: Before you take massive action to fight your plateau, make sure you are indeed stuck in the mud. Don't rely on your scale alone. Measure your body proportions with a measuring tape or calipers. Try on some clothes that used to be too tight. Count your belt loops. In short, track your size through a number of ways because there are times on keto when you drop a size without losing weight.

If you do make a dietary change to get off the plateau, test the results for a period of two to four weeks to see if works. If not, pivot to another approach. Take control of your health, researching and experimenting with what works for you.

Here are some actions you can take to spark up the weight loss again:

Fire up an exercise program: Any type of endurance training or high-intensity interval training (HIIT) improves glucose tolerance. It's not about burning calories as much as it is about kicking in your metabolism by building muscle. Muscle burns more fat.

Fix the problem fast...by fasting: I use intermittent fasting on a 16:8 schedule, which means fasting from 8 p.m. to noon. That means I go sixteen hours without eating and consume all meals during the remaining eight hours of the day. I have used this 16:8 fasting method often with great success. You may even decide to take a more aggressive stance with an alternate day feeding schedule. This is not necessarily a means of calorie restriction but a way of redistributing your calories in your schedule such that you are relying on fat reserves more often.

Cut the damn carbs: Another way to break the plateau cycle is to eat a nearly zero-carb diet that is 90 percent fat and restricted to little more than one thousand calories per day. Make sure you accurately count carbs and reduce your total caloric intake.

Be patient: All cells die and regenerate every seven years. This means every seven years you basically have a new body. It stands to reason that it could take a number of years for all the new cells to grow and reprogram while you maintain a ketogenic lifestyle. If you are disciplined and stick with it, your new cells with be more insulin sensitive than your old cells, and over time your homeostatic weight will drop.

CONCLUSION

FOLLOWING THE STOICS

I learned about stoicism through a Tim Ferriss podcast interview with Ryan Holiday, the author of *The Daily Stoic: 366 Meditations on Wisdom, Perseverance, and the Art of Living*. I read from this book every day. I recommend it to anybody struggling with discipline. Tim Ferriss, the author of *The 4-Hour Workweek* and other books, is a big follower of stoicism. He did a brilliant TED talk on it and often refers to stoicism and Marcus Aurelius in his podcast *The Tim Ferriss Show*. The central tenet of stoicism is the ability to endure hardship, pain, disappointment, sadness, and loss without displaying an overabundance of emotion. Another key tenet of this philosophy is that we all must have a loyalty to society and an obligation to help it.

That's one of the reasons I started my company. It's why I'm writing this book.

We all must find a way to pay it forward.

The more I learned about stoicism, the more I thought of my grandfather. He was a combination of the stoic and Zen master without even trying. He was the best man I've ever known. Everything about him was good. He had an amazing sense of humor. You could always count on him. I'd never met a more honest man. He passed away at age ninety-seven, and it's been tough because he was my role model more than anyone else in the world.

He did something odd for his time—he retired at age forty. He'd been a truck driver and had also owned a Christmas tree farm outside Green Bay, Wisconsin. I remember him getting up at 2 a.m. to drive trucks. On weekends when he wasn't driving, he'd go out to the tree farm and prune the trees and spray them for bugs. He saved every single penny and made smart investments. He built a cabin on Lake Oneonta in northern Wisconsin, and after he quit his job and sold the Christmas tree farm, he and my grandmother moved to the cabin to live full time. They were never wealthy. They had just enough. Even though he had retired so much earlier than most people, when I asked him if he had any regrets, he said, "I wish I hadn't worked so much." Sage advice from a beautiful, hardworking man.

Even in his nineties, he always shoveled the snow from his sidewalk and stairs. He always made sure there was food for the birds around his property. He lived in perfect harmony with nature and his surroundings. When company visited, he'd make his secret fried fish recipe from fish he'd caught in the lake. He was the chef in the house, and it was beautiful watching him prepare a meal. He was always completely present in any moment he was in, from chopping the carrots to flipping those pancakes made with his top-secret recipe.

I admired my grandfather's integrity more than anything. Here's an example that tells you everything: after he applied for social security and they started sending him checks, he actually tried to return them because he said he didn't need them.

He's the example I've tried to set for myself. I thought of him that day in Las Vegas when I woke up and took an honest look at myself—overweight, hung over, and living an overindulgent lifestyle while running a company designed to help people be healthy by fighting metabolic disease. His memory heightened the pain I felt. I lived a life of sloth and dishonesty. How could I be the leader of a company devoted to improving health when I was the one who needed help? I was disappointed in myself because I wasn't living up to my grandfather's standards for integrity.

Human beings change when the resulting pain of their actions exceeds the pleasure they derive from those actions and bad habits. That day in Vegas, my pain approached that threshold. Instead of suppressing that pain, I flooded myself with it in the hope that I'd reach the tipping point. I wanted to change, to leave a legacy my grandfather would be proud of.

That's when I decided I would not live like that another day. I made a choice and stuck with it. I changed my lifestyle, lost those thirty-five pounds, and got into the best shape of my life at fifty-seven.

Stoicism plays a vital role in my lifestyle choices. Stoicism requires that I look at my behavior from both the outside and the inside, and that my ethical compass points in the right direction.

Stoicism helps me make intelligent decisions because the philosophy teaches you to disregard emotion in your decision making. When you ignore needs and expectations, you're not disappointed if something blows up, fails, or doesn't deliver the results you planned. Stoicism gives you the ability to turn that outcome into an opportunity to learn and grow.

Stoicism discourages you from bragging about your accomplishments, or the pursuit of having more than anybody else. It guides me to a humble life, living within my means, and directing me to be generous and contribute to the community.

THIS IS IT

I'm a person of science and an atheist. I don't believe in heaven, hell, or ghosts. I've seen many friends, relatives, and a beloved pet die in the past three years, mostly of cancer. I lost both my parents and my grandfather. The scientist in me believes that once you die, that's it. Your life is over. Dead relatives aren't returning to visit me in my sleep. Their faces aren't showing up on a piece of toast. They're gone.

Still, I have a deep appreciation for my life. Buddhists say life is as rare as throwing a ring into the ocean and having it fall over the head of a sea turtle. Your life results from a convergence of remarkable events. One sperm outswims another sperm. Your parents make eye contact at the right moment. The odds of your life emerging from this confluence of fleeting events are astronomically long. I heard in a recent TED talk featuring Mel Robbins that the chance of you being alive in this world are four trillion to one. When you look at it this way, life feels like a gift. Life is a gift. Treasure every moment of it.

Not many people look at it that way, however. They see

life as a struggle. When I encounter people like this, I want to shake them, and say, "Hey, you're alive. You are alive! Do you realize how unlikely that is?" We all should be grateful for this astonishing intertwining of circumstances that creates us, and we should all take the best possible care of that temple that is our body.

If you inflict bad health on yourself by carrying more weight than your joints can handle or eating so much sugar that your gut chemistry is out of whack—you destroy the gift you've been given.

One of the quotes I live by (and which is on my personal stationery) is, "Dream like you'll live forever and live like you'll die tomorrow."

You have one life to live, and you'd better make it fucking great.

YOUR PATH FORWARD

With this book, I've sketched out a path you can take toward making your life better. I've described what worked for me, and I've given you some ideas about steps you can take to change your diet, change your habits, and change your lifestyle. How you go about your own journey—what exercise you start with, the type of meals you prepare—is up to you. But as you set forth, here is a recap of the key ideas to keep in mind:

"A GOAL NOT WRITTEN DOWN IS NOTHING BUT A GOOD INTENTION."

I heard that from Tony Robbins when I attended one of his seminars and did a fire walk in 1989. Since then, I've written my goals down every single year. I write them down in detail, specifying what I want the outcome to be, and why I want to achieve this goal. On New Year's Day each year, I review and reflect on those goals. When I decided to make a lifestyle change in October of 2016, I wrote down in my journal how I was going to do it and which day I was going to hit my target weight of 185 pounds. (I haven't hit that goal yet—I still have fifteen more pounds to go.)

FIND YOUR TRIBE

One of my dear influencers, Lewis Howes, has pounded into my head the importance of finding your tribe. I'm very close to my family, and when I made a lifestyle change, I told them I needed their support. You will need support, too, if you adopt a ketogenic lifestyle. As I mentioned, you are the sum of the five people you spend the most time with. If you aren't surrounded by people who support your lifestyle, you must find new friends. If you don't see a future with the person beside you, it may be time to choose another path.

CHANGE YOUR SHOULD TO MUST

In order to reach a goal, the goal has to be a must, or you could end up should-ing all over yourself. Shoulda, woulda, coulda. Look at the difference:

I should lose thirty-five pounds. (Meh, I'll get around to it one of these days.)

I must lose thirty-five pounds. (I'll start today!)

KEEP A GROWTH MINDSET

Remember the growth mindset versus the fixed mindset? A fixed mindset says you can't do it, that things will never change. A growth mindset says you can succeed, accomplish your goal, and adapt to change. Negative emotions can't coexist with a mindset of gratitude. You can't be grateful and depressed, or grateful and fearful, or grateful and angry at the same time. If you live in a state of gratitude, you avoid the fear, depression, anger, resentment, and sorrow that can creep into life. I don't want to harp on you, dear reader, but I highly recommend you pick up a copy of Carol Dweck's book *Mindset*. Really good stuff.

Stoics pivot when something isn't working for them. This includes relationships. If a friend or companion isn't supporting your lifestyle and personal growth, let them know. If they don't listen, reconsider how much time you spend with them.

LESSONS LEARNED FROM PAIN

Pain facilitates growth. Muscles sore from exercise recover to become stronger and more able to do more work. People facing mental stress adapt and learn to handle even higher levels of stress. People who feel the pain of regret can also adapt and can learn to avoid the things they previously regretted. Pain teaches us the power of endurance and perseverance.

Kobe Bryant is a good example. Kobe is considered by many to be one of the best all-around basketball players of all time, but he endured a lot of pain to reach that status. When he was a player, no one outworked Kobe Bryant. He hit the gym floor before anyone else and then stayed later than everyone else. Kobe became one of the best because of his willingness to out-suffer his opponents.

Pain and suffering are the most beautiful human conditions. Nothing fosters growth more effectively.

People are going to open up a can of nasty on me for saying

this. They're going to say, "What about those people in sub-Saharan Africa, starving and living under religious subjugation?" That is not what I'm talking about. I'm not talking about suffering injustice, although deep understanding often comes from that. Look at Nelson Mandela, imprisoned under apartheid, or Viktor Frankl, imprisoned under Nazi Germany. These men experienced intense levels of pain and suffering and emerged with insights that inspired millions of people. Viktor Frankl helped us remember the Holocaust. Nelson Mandela defeated apartheid and freed his people. What motivated them to pitch these battles and take on these immeasurable challenges? It was the pain they endured.

The contribution I'm hoping to make, and the purpose of this book, is to help people committing to a lifestyle change. When people follow the steps—to adapt, to pivot, to take pain and suffering and leverage it into personal growth—that is triumph, and triumph brings tears to my eyes. If that's the outcome, then this book will be the greatest success of my lifetime.

ARE YOU READY?

If you've made the decision to change, think of the keto-genic lifestyle as a journey and not a destination. Keep these things in mind:

- You will have some good days, and you will have some bad days.
- You will have days when you lose weight and some days when your weight ticks up.
- You will have days where you're frustrated and days when you're joyous.
- Embrace pain. Embrace failure. As a wise woman once told me, "Learn from your mistakes and grow from your failures." It is a gift that will propel you forward to change, success, and joy.

Above all else, collect data. Record that data in your journal every day. Make it a habit, a ritual. Complete data about yourself and your activities gives you a holistic view of your progress. You may not see yourself going down in clothing sizes, but you will see other indicators that you're on the right track. You'll see your blood pressure drop. You'll be able to do more reps, run more miles. You'll sleep better. You'll enjoy meals more.

KEY LESSONS

IT'S ABOUT BODY, MIND, AND SPIRIT

Food and exercise are the main strategies behind your success, but don't forget to connect your body to your mind and spirit. When you are connected to your body, you feel it when you eat something that's not good for you. Integrating diet, exercise, and some sort of relaxation or body therapy will help you succeed by lowering stress. Stress is a major cause of people overeating because they often comfort themselves with food. Here are some relaxation tips to use instead:

- Yoga helps get in touch with your body. It doesn't feel like vigorous exercise, but it gives you a good workout. It also reduces stress.
- Integrate some therapeutic massage. Massage stimulates the blood and lymphatic systems and also relaxes you. Get a massage once a month—or once a week if you can.
- Meditation is key to your success. It has benefits on so many levels. If you do focused breathing in your meditation, it allows your brain to connect with your body. The breathing then allows your mind to clear and grounds you to allow you to deal with stress much more effectively.
- Come from a place of gratitude. Tony Robbins says that "anger, sadness, or depression cannot coexist with gratitude." Stay in a state of gratitude and you will find that your worries will disappear. I keep a journal on my kitchen counter that I write in at the end of each day, always listing at least four things for which I am grateful.

Use this book as a guide, as a reference point to help you stay on track. Refer back to it if you find yourself slipping away from a ketogenic lifestyle. Let it remind you to commit to doing everything involved in a lifestyle change, such as paying attention to labels as you seek to cut hidden sugars from your food.

Follow the recipes in this book. They're all simple and delicious, and they'll help you lose weight.

YOUR PERSONAL VIRTUAL JUSTICE LEAGUE

This journey will be easier if you are part of a tribe of people that have adopted a ketogenic lifestyle. They'll understand what you go through. If people aren't available to be your circle of five, create your own virtual justice league. This is what I've done. I've got a team of influencers that I read, listen to, and watch on a regular basis. They're my superheroes.

- Dom D'Agostino is the foremost authority on the ketogenic lifestyle. He's a professor at the University of South Florida, and his knowledge is deep. Visit his website and read his blog. (https://dominicdagostino. wordpress.com/)
- Tim Ferriss (author of *The 4-Hour Workweek* and *Tools of Titans*, among others) is amazing. Read his books and listen to his podcasts.
- Rhonda Patrick delivers heady science stuff and is unbelievable. Her website is www.foundmyfitness.

com, and you can enjoy her podcasts there. I can listen to her for hours.

- Tom Bilyeu, the entrepreneur who cofounded Quest Nutrition, has an interview series where he examines the mindsets of the world's highest achievers to learn their secrets of success. Find it at https://impactthe-ory.com/.
- Carol Dweck of Stanford University is one of the world's leading authorities on motivation. Read her book *Mindset*.
- Lewis Howes, the former football player and founder of *The School of Greatness* talk show, always sends a positive message. You can find him at lewishowes.com.
- James Altucher, the tech entrepreneur and author of *Choose Yourself*, is inspiring and insightful with his ideas about stripping away all the unnecessary trappings of your life and focusing on the simple things that are most important to you. In fact, I was listening to Altucher's podcast with Tucker Max when I was inspired to write this book. Thanks, James! Thanks, Tucker! I never thought I could do it, but here it is, and people are reading it. Amazing.

ENVISION THE OUTCOME

You need to create a vision of your desired outcome. It's not a wish. It's not a hope. It's specific, concrete. Your brain doesn't know the difference between reality and a thought. Your brain believes that any thought is reality. If you're able to visualize what you want, your brain is already there. All you need to do is take the physical steps to manifest it. It's that easy.

Creating a vision board is a great way to kick-start this process. Cut out a picture of the body you've always wanted and put your face on it. If you're a digital person, there are apps for creating a virtual vision board (like DreamItAlive. com), but I prefer my vision board to be in physical form.

To give your creative visualization an extra boost, do it while meditating. Take some deep breaths and put yourself into state and visualize what that outcome is.

In addition, set down your concrete goals in your journal and establish timeframes for those goals. Where do you see yourself in six months or a year? If you think it, ink it. Write it down, periodically review it, and work every day at reaching that goal.

YOU ARE THE TROPHY

You're not going to win prizes or trophies at the end of this process. But you do get a healthy body. Here's what else you'll earn:

- Dignity

- Self-respect
- Confidence

These qualities are now part of you. You are the trophy.

WHAT TO DO WHEN YOU CLOSE THIS BOOK

- Check out my website, GuyGoneKeto.com. You'll find lots of great information there, including keto meal plans, testimonials, support groups, resources, and links to the latest science on ketogenesis.
- Get in touch. I want to know how you're doing, so leave a message on the website and share your story. Triumph brings tears to my eyes, so I want to hear all your success stories.

Remember, this is not a diet book.

Diets are temporary; lifestyles are long term. You won't have ongoing success with a diet. You'll lose weight, but you'll go off the diet and gain all the weight back and more. The weight going up and down is unhealthy, and you never enjoy a sense of satisfaction.

Instead, change your lifestyle. Think of this book as a lifestyle book and use it to help change your lifestyle.

EPILOGUE

Do you believe in serendipity? Well, neither do I. But I recently had an experience that made me rethink how I feel about happy coincidences.

Exactly one year from when I started this journey in the gross room at the Luxor after eating a massive meal and downing a few glasses of wine, I found myself in the same exact room at the same hotel. That evening I had dinner at the same restaurant with the same client I'd eaten with a year earlier.

Sitting at the table, my client remarked how much of a different person I had become. He could tell I'd lost weight and that I looked much fitter than I had the previous year. I still had a steak, but it was a much smaller portion than I'd had the previous year. I had a side of steamed broccoli, which I slathered with butter, and I even had a small glass of dry red wine. I skipped dessert and headed to my room to hit the sack early.

This time, when I looked in the mirror, I saw a completely different person. I saw a warrior. I saw triumph, and of course, tears welled up in my eyes.

ACKNOWLEDGEMENTS

They say a journey of a thousand miles starts with a single step, and every book starts with a single question. This was the case with me when I offered to take Ron Penna from Quest Nutrition out to dinner. (After all, Portland is such a foodie town.)

However, Ron demurred.

"I don't eat," he said.

"You don't eat?" I asked, mystified.

"No," he replied.

Well, I get it now, Ron: I used to make eating my focus, and food controlled my life. Now I control what I put in my body, and it shows. I have so, so much to thank Ron

Penna for: he has been largely responsible for putting my business on the fast track to success. I also thank Ron for setting me on course through his Spartan ways. I eat to live, rather than living to eat.

I want to thank my loving sisters, Gina King and Jill Casey. They are beautiful, loving, and supportive. Above all, they call me out on my crap. I love you guys. This wouldn't have been possible without your love and support.

Thank you to Lisa "Hammer" Sheridan and Ryan "Kubster" Flowers. They kept the ship moving in the right direction while I dove into writing this book. Also, I would be remiss in not mentioning Ethan Jeffries, our resident keto kid, who has been the subject of many an experiment.

Thank you, Cheryl Tessier, my public relations guru. You have always been supportive and such a good listener. It is a pleasure working with you.

I want to thank Jim Sloan, Emily Gindlesparger, Kevin Murphy, Tucker Max, and the entire team at Book in a Box. You guys have been amazing to work with. You brought my words together in a way that perfectly represents my passion for a ketogenic lifestyle. I can't wait to work with your team again on my next book. You made this a blast.

It is said that you are the sum of the five people closest to you. It is an honor for me to have these fine folks in my inner circle.

ABOUT THE AUTHOR

THOMAS J. KING is the founder and CEO of Steviva Brands Inc., one of the largest importers, manufacturers, and distributors of natural sweeteners. A self-described bio hacker, he has made it his life's work to study food science and use his knowledge to help people eat healthier, avoid harmful sugars, and maintain diet and exercise habits that defeat metabolic disease. His company, based in Portland, Oregon, derives its name from stevia, the South American plant extract that is calorie-free yet three hundred times sweeter than sugar and that does not contribute to the combination of maladies that Thom calls "diabesity."